MOLLY
HALL
April 27, 2000
Feathered Friends Birthday Club

THE NEW GUIDE TO
Junior Showmanship

Junior Showmanship, the future of the dog sport, provides a great variety of experiences for young people and dogs of any age. *Photo by Michael Baker*

THE NEW GUIDE TO
Junior
Showmanship

Connie Vanacore

HOWELL BOOK HOUSE

New York

Maxwell Macmillan Canada
Toronto

Maxwell Macmillan International
New York   Oxford   Singapore   Sydney

Howell Book House   Maxwell Macmillan Canada, Inc.
Macmillan Publishing Company   1200 Eglinton Avenue East
866 Third Avenue   Suite 200
New York, NY 10022   Don Mills, Ontario M3C 3N1

Macmillan Publishing Company is part of the Maxwell Communication Group of Companies.

Library of Congress Cataloging-in-Publication Data

Vanacore, Connie.
    The new guide to junior showmanship/Connie Vanacore.
        p.   cm.
    Includes bibliographical references (p. 173) and index.
    ISBN 0-87605-653-2
    1. Dog shows—Junior showmanship classes—Juvenile
literature.   2. Dogs—Juvenile literature.   [1. Dogs—
Showing.   2. Dogs.]   I. Title.
    SF425.13.V36   1994
    636.7'0888—dc20   93–48059
                                                                CIP
                                                                AC

Macmillan books are available at special discounts for bulk purchases for sales promotions, premiums, fund-raising, or educational use. For details, contact:

                          Special Sales Director
                          Macmillan Publishing Company
                          866 Third Avenue
                          New York, NY 10022

10 9 8 7 6 5 4 3 2 1

Printed in the United States of America

For Jessica, Tara and Michael
who love dogs because they are dogs

Contents

13. Giving Something Back **155**

Foreword

ONE OF THE MOST IMPORTANT activities in the sport of dogs is Junior Showmanship. Because of my belief in the principles upon which it was established, I am delighted that Connie Vanacore has written *The New Guide to Junior Showmanship*.

Junior Showmanship competition serves as a foundation for and affects the future of the sport in many ways. This is an activity that involves, trains and produces young people who hopefully remain in the dog show world as participants and contributors. Breeders, exhibitors, handlers and judges have come from the ranks of Junior Showmanship. As a result, Junior Showmanship often produces the future leaders in the sport of dogs.

Involvement in Junior Showmanship also builds the skills that enhance and affect the futures of these youngsters. By profession I am a guidance counselor in the Connecticut school system. As an educator and a dog show judge, I have discovered that the lessons and values young people learn while participating in Junior Showmanship help mold their lives and are invaluable to them as adults.

Through this activity they learn how to show a dog, how to win and lose gracefully, how to compete in an emotionally healthy way, how to work with and appreciate others and how to be a responsible dog owner. While increasing their skills, they gain in self-confidence, develop the ability to perform in front of others and grow in their appreciation of the rewards of hard work.

This book, written in language young people can understand, is an excellent source and resource for anyone who wants to participate in or understand more about Junior Showmanship. The author's ability to write about this and other pertinent areas of our sport comes from her almost forty years' involvement in dogs. She has been active as an exhibitor, an occasional breeder, a member and officer of breed and all-breed clubs and as a Delegate to the American Kennel Club. Connie Vanacore has said that becoming a writer grew from her involvement in the sport of dogs and is an example of how one's hobby can become a rewarding occupation. She notes that her time spent in this avocation has been a love affair both with her dogs and with the people who have become her closest friends.

The New Guide to Junior Showmanship is an important gift to the young participants and future leaders of this sport that we love.

Patricia Laurans
AKC Delegate
German Wirehaired Pointer
Club of America

Introduction

JUNIOR SHOWMANSHIP classes evolved as part of the concept of dog shows as family sport and entertainment. They were conceived in the 1930s and have grown in participation and importance until, today, they are an integral part of almost every dog show held in the United States and in many countries around the world.

Junior Showmanship would not exist without the interest of young people in learning to care for, train and compete in the show ring with their dogs. The adage that children and dogs belong together is not always true. In some instances a natural affinity will exist between a particular dog and a child, but in many circumstances the relationship between them must be learned and earned. Children can be impatient, intolerant and sometimes cruel, either knowingly or as a result of ignorance, to animals. Dogs can be rough, demanding, annoying, fearful or bossy with kids.

Understanding each other takes time and the knowledge of what to expect and what is expected from the other. Communication between a person and a dog develops through learned behavior. Just as a child learns the alphabet and then learns to read, a dog must be taught the words, phrases and gestures that enable that dog to

This puppy and Junior get to know each other.

understand the owner or handler's expectations. A child must learn
how to communicate with a dog through methods that a dog can
understand. In turn, the child must learn how to understand the dog
in order to create the teamwork necessary for a happy relationship
and a good working partnership.

TEAMWORK

Junior Showmanship involves teamwork just as much as any
team sport, whether baseball, soccer, football or basketball. Team-
mates rely on one another. Each team member plays his or her part.

In the Junior Showmanship ring the dog and the handler also
rely on each other to present the perfect picture to the judge. The
dog relies on the handler for guidance in all areas. The handler relies
on the dog to obey with willingness and style. The moves in the

Junior Showmanship ring are no less stylized and predictable than those on the playing field. They take as much practice and coordination, but before the practice can begin each must understand what must be learned and how to go about it.

Junior Showmanship is a way for dogs and kids to get together as part of an organized competitive sport which can involve the whole family. *The family dog becomes a vital part of the experience, rather than an adjunct or an afterthought.*

Through competition in the show ring, Juniors learn sportsmanship, how to win and lose gracefully, how to take responsibility for themselves and for the care of the dogs and how to enjoy a sport which gives thousands of people each year the joy of being a team with a special dog.

This book will help you to learn what Junior Showmanship is, how to understand the basic moves and how to become a winning combination with your dog.

Jane Forsyth, a former Junior Handler and then highly successful professional handler, is now a busy judge of many breeds.

1

The History of Junior Showmanship

J UNIOR SHOWMANSHIP has a venerable history. Its founder was Leonard Brumby, Sr., of Westbury, Long Island, New York. Mr. Brumby was a professional handler and kennel manager for a prestigious Terrier kennel in Westbury until he became a Vice-President of the American Kennel Club. He began the first children's handling classes at Westbury Kennel Club in 1932 for boys and girls under fourteen years of age.

In 1933, Westminster Kennel Club offered a children's handling championship class with the qualification that a child must have won a first place ribbon during the year.

In 1949, the Professional Handlers Association offered the Leonard Brumby, Sr., Memorial Trophy to be given each year at Westminster for the Best Junior Handler, and in 1951, classes for Juniors were changed from children's handling classes to Junior Showmanship.

Junior classes were originally judged by celebrities, movie stars or anyone interested in judging them. The Professional Handlers Association encouraged its members to judge and during this period the makeup of the classes was enlarged to Novice Junior, Open Junior, Novice Senior and Open Senior. Children aged ten to eighteen were eligible to compete.

In 1971, the American Kennel Club officially recognized Junior Showmanship. Former Juniors were encouraged to apply to judge, and in 1977, only those persons who were approved as conformation judges and Junior Showmanship–only judges could judge AKC Junior Showmanship competition. In 1992, these rules were revised to permit professional handlers to apply to judge Junior Showmanship without the necessity of relinquishing their handling occupation.

In 1989, the rules for judging Junior Showmanship were revised by a committee appointed by AKC which included prominent Junior competitors of the past. Several of these members are still active as judges, professional handlers or executives at the American Kennel Club.

It is interesting to learn about some of their experiences as Juniors and the role that experience plays in their lives today.

Most of the successful Juniors of the past and many of those active in Juniors in the 1990s acquired their interest in the sport through the participation of their parents. Anne Rogers Clark's mother was a prominent breeder of Poodles. Anne was practically born in a whelping box and was under the grooming tent helping her mother by the age of six. Jane Kamp Forsyth was also the child of a dog show family, as was George Alston, the former professional handler, whose mother raised Boxers. Two of the Alston children, Lisa Jane and Jennifer, are both handlers.

Mari Beth O'Neill's family raised and showed Doberman Pinschers and Mari Beth's first dog was a Manchester Terrier, part of the Pinscher family but small enough for a child to handle. Her father, Charles A. T. O'Neill, was the Executive Vice-President of the American Kennel Club until his retirement in the 1980s.

Bonnie Threlfall, her sister, Patty, and brother, Scott, came through the ranks as children of dog show parents. Bonnie's father, Harry Proctor, was a breeder of Labrador Retrievers. He enjoyed the Obedience ring, leaving the handling to the children. All three have become successful breeders and professional handlers.

It is not necessary to come from a dog show family in order to participate in the sport, but an early association with how dog shows work is an advantage to Juniors who have had that experience.

6

Some of those who came through the ranks of Junior Showmanship have remained in the sport as professional handlers or in other careers. Many have maintained their interest in Junior competition as teachers, or in other related careers. They have definite opinions on the way Juniors should conduct themselves in the ring and outside, and also how judges can contribute to the sport when they officiate in the Junior ring.

George Alston, a retired professional handler, gives seminars and classes in which Juniors may participate. In his opinion, the most important attribute a Junior can cultivate is "quiet hands." The dog should stand out more than the Junior, and the Junior (or any handler) should be almost invisible. Working as a team, rather than Junior against the dog, will give the impression that the handler is in control of the dog and that the two present a picture together. Mr. Alston's pet peeve is a handler, whether Junior or adult, who is in constant eye contact with the judge. Never try to stare down

Mary Ann Alston, who was a professional handler and is the mother of a former Junior, is now a judge, handing out the ribbons in a Junior Showmanship class.

(Photo by Michael Baker)

the judge, Mr. Alston says, and that consideration is echoed by other professionals, including Mary Ann Alston, his wife and a former professional handler, who is a Junior Showmanship judge as well as a conformation judge.

Mary Ann says that Juniors need to be aware of what the judge is doing, but should not maintain constant eye contact. Both Mary Ann and Jane Forsyth feel that Juniors need to be interested enough to notice what the judge is doing so they can follow instructions. Many Juniors do not listen, and therefore are penalized for *not* doing what the judge tells them to do. Judges must be consistent in treating every child the same, so the Juniors will know, if they are paying attention, what pattern the judge is asking for and when they will be required to set their dogs up for examination.

Jane Forsyth is interested to see how Juniors work with their dogs. Do they put effort into making a picture? Do they have good hands in the way they manage their dogs?

Mary Ann Alston wants to see Juniors who put the welfare of their dogs first. She wants to know that the Juniors are concerned with the physical and mental condition of their dogs. Handlers should be in control of their dogs at all times. They should show common sense about keeping their dogs in the shade on a hot day, keeping them away from bothering other dogs in the ring.

Bonnie Threlfall said that she learned a great deal about dog showing through her participation in Juniors. Much of what she learned came from the professional handlers who judged Junior classes. In those days, Junior Showmanship was a much less structured activity than it is today. Handlers who had some free time were pressed into service in any vacant ring, and they were not hesitant about teaching a young person how to do it better.

Showing is a small part of learning how to present a dog, Bonnie said. The best way to learn is to work for a reputable professional handler. If she were judging, Bonnie would look for the handler who is inconspicuous. She wants to notice the dog, not what the handler (Junior) is wearing or doing to attract attention. Her advice is to dress conservatively, don't chew gum or wear slippery shoes.

Juniors who might consider professional handling as a career should work for someone else for at least ten years. By that time they will know if they are really committed.

Bonnie acknowledged that showing in Juniors has some benefits, such as acquiring poise, attitude and self-confidence, but, she said, a child can take up ballet or give a recital to learn those skills, without putting the life of a dog at risk.

Many former Juniors were completely responsible for their dogs. Wayne Cavanaugh and Mari Beth O'Neill, both of whom went on to careers as executives with the American Kennel Club, were completely in charge of their dogs. They learned their commitment to the sport by learning to care for their own dogs—grooming, feeding, bathing, trimming and, least of all, presentation in the show ring. Wayne says that he learned respect for his dogs and for the sport because of the responsibility his parents gave him. In the old days, he says, children did not go into the ring with top winning dogs. They learned on the family pet at the same time they were learning about the sport. As a sport, it was less competitive than it is today. In those days, children were asked to switch dogs in the ring, in order to see how well they could handle something other than their own.

Wayne's father insisted that school grades came first. If grades fell, he was not allowed to show, but if he did show his dog, it also had to be shown by him in the breed on the same day. One of his

Wayne Cavanaugh, in a photo taken during his Junior days, is now an executive at the American Kennel Club.

greatest achievements was to win in Junior Showmanship with his English Setter and then to take Best of Breed from American-Bred class on the same day. He was twelve years old at the time and lost his armband in the Group ring. The judge kindly picked it up and returned it to him, a gesture of kindness that a nervous boy remembered.

Mari Beth O'Neill says that Junior Showmanship gave her the self-confidence to compete with other children and with adults in the show ring.

Lisa Agresta comes from a show-going family of Labrador Retriever fanciers. She and her three sisters were all in Junior Showmanship competition. She feels that the pressure is more intense in today's competition, and as a judge she tries to offset the jitters.

Lisa Agresta, a former Junior Handler who is now a judge, examines a Bichon Frisé being handled in a Junior Showmanship class.

She gathers her classes together before she begins to judge. She tells them exactly what she is going to do, and asks them to relax their dogs when they are not being examined. She wants to see Junior handlers with style, who present a dog as it would be shown in the conformation ring. Both she and Jane Forsyth want to see the handlers "make a picture" with their hands and the way they control their dogs.

All the former Juniors say their most valuable lessons were to learn sportsmanship, to be happy and humble when you win and to be happy and supportive of your competitors when they win. Camaraderie and lasting friendships are also benefits of competing in Junior Showmanship.

Parents can contribute to these attitudes by their own actions. Many children are too dependent on their parents for ringside instructions, Mary Ann Alston says, and conversely, some parents interfere by coaching from the sidelines. Unpleasantness in or outside the ring is something which Lisa Agresta will not forgive. Mari Beth says that it is important to show the dog, not yourself. George Alston's favorite phrase is "the best handler is invisible." All of the former exhibitors emphasize in one way or another that the dog comes first, in presentation, in care and in responsibility.

Through the years, the most successful professionals in the sport of dogs were Juniors who learned how to care for and be responsible for their own dogs. The great professional handlers such as Jane and Bob Forsyth, Bill Trainor and Terrier specialist George Ward taught generations of youngsters how to be good, responsible custodians of the dogs in their care at the same time as they were learning how to handle a variety of dogs.

For the vast majority of Juniors who became successful over time in the sport, one principle stands out: *The dog comes first—* and it is the Junior's responsibility to abide by that rule.

Getting acquainted with a Papillon. Will this be the breed she will choose?

2

Acquiring a Puppy

IN THE LAST CHAPTER we talked of the advantages of being born into a family associated with pure-bred dogs and dog shows. However, this is not a requirement for participation in the sport. In fact, the ability of Juniors to decide upon the breed of dog they most desire and the fun of finding the right dog for you is a big plus. You will learn a great deal about dogs by going to shows and watching the different breeds being judged, as well as by watching the Junior Showmanship classes.

THE FAMILY PET

Most families buy a dog because they want a nice pet to be part of their household. Juniors should remember that the show career of a dog is very short, only two or three years in most cases, but that dog will be part of the family for many years thereafter. It is important, therefore, that the fit between the dog and the family is a positive one. It is not enough for young people to promise faithfully to care for all the needs of a dog and then expect mom or dad to exercise, feed, groom and do all the other work involved in caring for a pet. Buying a dog should be a family decision and parents should also realize that as faithful as a child will try to be in living up to the responsibility of taking care of a pet, the demands of school, homework and other hobbies and activities will often interfere with that commitment. That is why everyone must be involved, not only in the choice of a pet but in the desire to own it and care for it. The family dog is truly the family's responsibility, even though the child may be nominal owner.

One also has to consider the fact that Juniors, until they reach their upper teen years, do not drive, so it will fall upon the parents to drive their children to shows, or to arrange for reliable transportation with friends for young handlers. Dog showing becomes a family recreation almost by default in some instances, but it can be among the most enjoyable of all pastimes.

THE RULES

AKC rules state that the dog a Junior shows must be owned by the Junior Handler or by the Junior Handler's father, mother, brother, sister, uncle, aunt, grandfather or grandmother, including the corresponding step and half relations, or by a member of the Junior Handler's household. That's a pretty broad category, but it does not mean that just anyone can hand off a dog to a Junior to take into the ring.

In addition, every dog entered for Junior Showmanship must be eligible to compete in Dog Show *or* Obedience Trials. This means that the dog must be AKC registered and purebred. It does not mean, however, that the dog must be of top show quality. The rules specifically state that *judges in the Junior Showmanship ring must not judge on the quality of the dog*, but only on the ability of the Junior to handle that dog according to the way it would be handled *if* it were shown in the breed ring. Different breeds are shown differently, and both the Junior and the judge must know how that particular breed should be exhibited. For example, if it is a small dog examined on the table in the conformation ring, then it should be shown the same way in Junior Showmanship. A breed such as a Collie is usually shown free-baited in the show ring. The Junior must learn how to show that dog properly in Junior competition.

14

Some breeds, such as the Afghan Hounds, are more glamorous than others and the temptation might be for a Junior to buy a breed which will, by itself, catch the judge's eye. This is never a good reason to buy into a breed.

You and your family should only decide which breed to buy after concluding that you really love it. The dog must be appropriate for *your* life and your own reasonable expectations of care and temperament. Judges will find competent handlers no matter what breeds they show. To be successful in Juniors, the fit and bond between dog and person must be right, whether it be a Miniature Pinscher or a Great Dane.

HOW TO CHOOSE A DOG TO SHOW

Showing dogs by definition means that you are going to buy a purebred and chances are that the dog will be a puppy. Where do you start? The first thing to decide is whether a big dog or a small dog is best. *What size are you?* If you are a small child you might

This young man is showing that his Afghan Hound is ready for the judge.

A young girl with a large Borzoi is showing her dog's head to the judge.

Two young Juniors with Bichons Frisés, waiting for the judge.

not want to start off with a dog that will grow to be 150 pounds and taller than you are. One of the rules states that Juniors must be able to control their dogs at all times, so it is a good idea to select a breed that fits your stature as you are growing.

Another factor is *the size of the home* you live in. If your family lives in an apartment you might not want a dog that needs lots of exercise and running. If these high-energy types don't get enough outdoor activity, they become real nuisances in the house. On the other hand, if you live in a house with a good-sized fenced yard, a dog that loves to be out playing may be just right for you.

The third thing for you and your family to consider is *grooming*. How much time do you have to brush and comb your pet every day? Since your dog will be primarily *your* responsibility, even though your parents may pitch in and help, too, the grooming chores should properly and mostly belong to you. You may love the look of a long-haired dog like a Golden Retriever or a Yorkshire Terrier, but realistically a short-haired breed such as a Boxer or a Pointer might be more appropriate. That is one of the decisions that you and your family must make and it will help narrow down the choice.

With 136 registered breeds to choose from, there is a breed for every taste and lifestyle, so you should take your time to select the one which suits you and your family best. One way to begin this task is to make a list of all the traits that you like and all the ones that you don't like. This should include things such as temperament, size, short- or long-haired and exercise requirements. Parents' preferences should also be included in this list. There are a few very popular dogs. Those in the top ten on AKC's registration list are fairly easy to find. Those others that are much less well known will require some research on your part to locate. There are many breeds that are not up on the popularity scale that make excellent pets and are very worthwhile investigating.

The library or your local bookstore is a good jumping off place for your search for the perfect dog. *The Complete Dog Book* (Howell Book House), the official publication of the American Kennel Club, describes every breed by background and official Standard for the breed. There are pictures of every breed, so you will have an idea what each looks like.

Once you have decided on a few breeds that you would like to consider, you have to see them. The best place to do that is at a dog show. Many sections of the country have shows somewhere within driving distance almost every weekend. The American Kennel Club (51 Madison Avenue, New York, NY 10010) can provide you with a list of all the show-giving clubs and the names of the people in charge. You can select a few in your area and find out when their shows are being held. Then you should go and plan to spend the day walking around, looking at the dogs.

Most of the shows are unbenched. This means that the dogs will be on the show grounds before that breed is judged, but most will go home after the judging, so you will not be able to see many of them if you arrive late. You can find out when the breeds you are interested in are being judged by your contact in the club. There are very few shows in the United States which are "benched." This means dogs have assigned places to stay when they are not being judged and must be present for a specific period of time so that people can see them throughout the day. A few of the benched shows still remaining are Westminster in New York, Detroit Kennel Club in Michigan, Kennel Club of Philadelphia in Pennsylvania and Golden Gate Kennel Club in San Francisco. It used to be that all shows were benched, but the cost to the clubs and convenience to exhibitors have made the benched show almost obsolete. In one way that is unfortunate, because at a benched show there is unlimited opportunity for the exhibitors to exchange information and ideas.

Most shows have Junior Showmanship competition, and you can find out from the same source when these classes are scheduled to be judged. You should watch a few classes to get an idea of the procedures of Junior Showmanship before venturing into the ring yourself.

If you are having difficulty finding a show to attend in your area, you might consider other steps first. After you have read *The Complete Dog Book*, or some other books which describe the many breeds available, select your favorites and contact the American Kennel Club to see if a video has been made about those breeds. These are available for purchase. Some local kennel clubs have them available for rental. You may also get a list of breeders in your area through the American Kennel Club or any local all-breed club. In addition, some states have federations to which most Specialty clubs and all-breed clubs belong. These organizations have lists of breeders they can send you. Another way to locate breeders is to contact all the local veterinarians. Some of them may have clients with those breeds to whom you can be referred.

It is important to visit several breeders of any of the breeds you are considering, so you can compare the dogs, the people and how the animals are kept. You will want to buy a puppy that is healthy and sound with a good pedigree. You should want to know as much as possible about the breed and its unique characteristics before you make your choice. You are also buying the breeder's knowledge.

All puppies are adorable, but you must look at the adults to see what your cute little creature will grow up to be. There is an old saying that before a boy marries a girl he had better look at her mother, because that is what his beautiful bride will become. The same holds true for puppies and adult dogs. If you are not entranced with the end result, don't buy the puppy.

Visiting a litter of Irish Setter puppies at the breeder's. Everyone is having a good time.

EVALUATING A LITTER

Let's move on to the next step. You have finally determined that a particular breed is right for you and your family. You have read the books, gone to one or two shows, met a few of the exhibitors and breeders and have found out who in your general area breeds those dogs. In a stroke of luck, you have discovered that one or two have litters of puppies.

Call and inquire about the puppies. Start by asking whether any are available, how old they are and whether they are males or females (whichever sex interests you). Ask if you may come to see the puppies. *Do not start off by asking the price.* Nothing turns a breeder off faster than that question at the outset. Of course, you are going to want to know whether you can afford the puppy, but if that's your first consideration, many breeders will not go any further. In fact, sometimes breeders will adjust their price once they have met you, if they feel that you will provide a wonderful home for their dog. You'll never know that, however, if your first approach is a big turn-off to them.

If the breeder says that the puppies are old enough to be seen (usually six weeks or older, after they have had their first vaccination) make an appointment and be on time. *Be prepared to answer a lot of questions from the breeder.* Reputable breeders put a lot of time, energy and money into their puppies, and they want to make sure the homes they go to are just right. They want to know that you are serious about this dog. They want to be sure that you realize that a dog is a long-term commitment and that you and your family will be there to care for it after you have gone off to college or to a job or out on your own. Dogs are never out on their own. They are always home, like dependent children, and careful breeders try to make people understand that before they buy their puppies.

Here are some of the things they will ask you, and you should be prepared to answer *before* you go looking for a dog:

- Who will be responsible for caring for the dog?
- Who will be responsible for feeding, exercising, bathing and grooming as well as taking the dog to the vet for shots and check-ups?
- Who will play with it and train it to be a good house companion?

20

- Where will the dog live?
- Will the pup be in the house with the family, in part of the house or in a kennel outside?
- Will it be exercised on a leash, in a fenced yard or in a kennel run?
- Who will care for your dog during the day when you are in school?
- *Does everyone in the family want this dog?*

Buyers have questions, too, and good breeders are usually happy to answer them and tell you all about their puppies. You will want to know if the puppies are registrable with AKC and you will want to see their pedigree. You might want to see pictures of the sire, which often is owned by someone else, and you'll want to see the dam of the puppies.

Look around to see how the puppies are kept. Are they clean, sturdy, bright-eyed, friendly. They should have shiny coats and feel warm and firm to the touch. Puppies should not feel clammy or damp. Their eyes and noses should not be runny and their skin should be clean with no evidence of crusts, scale or any parasites. They should have that sweet, distinctive puppy odor.

You should ask about vaccinations and feeding schedules. The breeder should provide you with lots of information about how to care for your puppy. If you agree on the purchase the breeder should give you registration documents, vaccination certificates and dates on which the puppy should receive the remainder of its shots. Often breeders will provide a sack of food to start you off so that the puppy can stay on the food which it has been fed. This is to avoid stomach upsets, and you should plan to stay on the same diet, at least for a while.

Puppies have individual personalities, which are obvious at a very young age. Some are born leaders, others followers. Some are outgoing, noisy and bossy. Others are like wallflowers at a dance who sit off to the side waiting for someone to notice them. Good breeders will usually try to match dogs to the families who are going to own them. After talking to you and your family a breeder may suggest a puppy in the litter which would be most suitable for you. The breeder might feel that a particular puppy, either boy or girl, would be the best companion, even though you may have decided in advance that one sex or the other is preferable. Bear in mind that

Can you spot the leaders in this group?

in order to compete in regular conformation classes, dogs and bitches may not be altered, except in the Veterans classes, even though they are eligible for Junior Showmanship. Most important, bitches in season may not compete in Junior Showmanship classes. You might wish to consider this when deciding on which sex to own.

PARENTAL RESPONSIBILITY

Here's a word for parents. In all likelihood, you will accompany your son or daughter to look at the puppies and to aid in the decision and in the purchase of this addition to the family. As far as practical, allow your child to be the primary focus in the negotiations between your family and the breeder. Breeders are impressed with youngsters who show some maturity and willingness to take responsibility for this creature.

Keep in mind, however, that no matter what promises are made by children to abide by their vows, the fallback has to be the parent. No puppy or adult dog should suffer neglect because the children are not mature enough to live up to their responsibilities. The parents absolutely have to want this dog. Some breeders feel so strongly about this that they will not sell a puppy to a family which states that it will be the child's dog exclusively. They know from experience that the dog has just bought a round-trip ticket back to the breeder in those circumstances.

It is a fine line between allowing children to exercise responsibility at their own pace and a parent stepping in when the puppy is in need of care, feeding and attention. Insisting that the child walk, feed, groom and care for the puppy often leads to the puppy being left alone and neglected while the child is at school or off at activities.

Children who decide that they wish to participate in Junior Showmanship have to make a great many choices concerning their free time. Since shows are held on weekends, in some areas of the country within driving distance every weekend, choices between sports, social events and school projects must be made in advance. One cannot decide to be a member of the varsity soccer team *and* expect to also go to dog shows *every* week. Teens, especially, find the decisions to be quite difficult as activities multiply.

Parents, too, must be willing to give up their weekend activities in order to take their children to the shows. This is the principal reason why so many Juniors come from families whose weekend hobby or profession is centered around dog shows. Parents are there anyway, with or without their children. Often, in order to keep the children interested and involved in the family pastime, they are given a dog of their own to show.

Regardless of how the child comes to own a dog, it ultimately becomes the parents' responsibility, *as well as the child's,* to care for and nurture the animal.

A parent's role does not end with buying the food, chauffeuring to the vet, cleaning up after the puppy and, in general, acting as a surrogate parent. He or she must also supervise the training of the puppy and guide the inexperienced and often impatient child in the correct way to relate to a dog. It may involve taking the child and the dog to Obedience or show handling classes at night. It may mean giving friendly advice on how best to show the puppy. It may involve intervention if the child becomes frustrated and angry because the puppy does not perform well. It is up to the parent to forbid a

A Junior Handler gaiting her Yorkshire Terrier at the proper speed.

child to abuse a puppy for any reason, under any circumstances whatsoever.

The parent may have to learn about dog showing along with the child, if both are entering this sport for the first time. Handling classes, seminars, reading books, watching exhibitors at shows— all are good ways to learn about dog shows. Here is another way that the breeder of your puppy can be an invaluable source of information and assistance. Parents should resist the temptation, however, of taking the puppy away from the child. Parents too often transform the learning experience for the child into the adult's single-minded quest for a ribbon for the dog.

This Junior stacks her Bichon Frisé on the table.

Remember, Junior Showmanship is judged on the performance of the child in the ring, not on the dog. For this reason, it is better to forget about the conformation ring while the child is showing in Juniors. Conflicts often arise when Junior Handlers are supposed to be in the ring at the same time that the breed conformation or Obedience class is called. There have been some very disappointed youngsters whose parents have opted to forget about them in order to take the dog into conformation instead.

That gambit is a sure way to cause a child to lose interest in a hurry. Better to enter the dog in Junior Showmanship competition and breed competition at different shows if an agreement cannot be reached *in advance* about which takes precedence.

Finally, there will come a time when your child is ready to go off to college, move to whatever state is in fashion at the time or get married. The dog that you bought for your child and that has grown up in your family may be left behind, no longer a puppy but an aging pet. Although it seems far in the future, the years go by rapidly, and parents end up with independent offspring but a very dependent pet.

Juniors are usually proud to have a dog of their own and to take responsibility for it, if they are guided and helped by understanding and sympathetic parents. The whole experience can be a positive one if handled correctly from the beginning. That is why it is so important that parents are willing and able to care for this new member of the family.

3

Growing Up
with Your Puppy

THE EARLY MONTHS of a puppy's life are most important for its emotional development. Whether you bought a puppy from a breeder, or whether your family bred the litter, the associations experienced during the impressionable first eight to twelve weeks of life will influence the development of the puppy's potential to be a wonderful pet or just an average dog.

At birth, a puppy's primary association is with the mother and any littermates. Food, sleep and warmth are all any puppy needs for the first three weeks of life. A good brood bitch will take care of her puppies with little help from the breeder, aside from keeping the brood bitch clean and well fed.

Once the puppies begin to move about and once their eyes and ears open to the world, various outside stimuli can be introduced. Normal household noise, radios, doors shutting, vacuum cleaners humming, telephones ringing should become a part of the puppies' experiences, because this is the world they will live in when they grow up.

The dam will usually wean the puppies herself, often by six

weeks of age. Sometimes breeders will wean them earlier and certainly begin to feed them solid food at about four weeks of age. If you buy a puppy, chances are that you will not be permitted to take your pup from the litter until it is at least eight weeks old. Often breeders hold on to their best puppies longer than that, but if you and your parents are able to convince the breeder that you will provide the best of care, you may be able to take your puppy home after the litter has received the first vaccinations.

THE NEW ARRIVAL AT HOME

It is important for the health of the puppy that you follow the breeder's recommendations on feeding your puppy. Abrupt changes in diet will cause diarrhea. Puppies will eat four times a day from the time they are eight weeks old until they are about four months. At that point, food can be given three times a day. Gradually, the puppy will pass up a meal on its own, usually the midday feeding, so you can reduce the number to twice a day from about nine months on. Many people feed twice a day as a permanent routine, believing

This proud Irish Setter mother takes care of her litter until it is about six weeks old.

that it is better for the dog to receive two smaller portions, rather than one large meal. This is especially important for the big breeds, which are prone to a gastric disturbance known as bloat. Bloat is considered a true veterinary emergency, as death can result if the stomach twists on itself. This is known as gastric torsion and results in death if not corrected quickly because the blood supply to the area is shut off.

If you decide to change foods after you have had your puppy home for a couple of weeks, do so gradually to minimize upsets, and be observant so that you can determine whether the puppy is growing at a steady rate and is utilizing the food well. Not every brand of the dozens on the market will agree with every dog. Once you find the one that seems to suit your dog, stay with it. Small breed dogs have higher caloric needs than the larger breeds and may be kept on puppy food until they are a year old. Many veterinarians, in response to feeding studies, recommend that the large breeds be changed over to adult food at about four months. This is so the growth rate is slowed to allow the bones to calcify properly and to avoid the bone diseases which some feel are caused by overnutrition in the rapidly growing breeds. Your puppy should be fed a balanced diet but will not need extra supplements if what you are feeding is a complete diet.

TRAINING YOUR PUPPY

Puppies need sleep, food, warmth and companionship in order to grow up mentally and physically healthy. They need to play and explore their new surroundings, and should be exposed to a variety of sights and sounds as they grow up.

You can help your puppy develop an attitude of confidence by including the new arrival in your activities. Once the pup's series of vaccinations have been completed, at about twenty weeks, you can feel secure in taking the puppy for walks, to the shopping center or to the park, where your dog will meet people and other dogs. You will be teaching the pup to walk on a lead and to obey some of the basic Obedience commands. Puppies learn very quickly and will respond to both your spoken and unspoken commands. You can teach a puppy to sit, to follow you and to come when called if

Companionship means sharing the couch with an English Cocker Spaniel.

you do this every day for a short period of time and *with plenty of praise and hugs*. There are many how-to training books, and you might even decide to enroll the puppy in a Kindergarten Puppy Training class. The most important thing to remember is to *always make it fun for both of you* and always make it an upbeat experience. You know how you feel when the teacher yells at you for making a mistake but never acknowledges when you've done something good. Well, puppies react the same way. They want to please you and they need your love.

Patience

One of the hardest things for Juniors to learn is patience, and yet that quality will get you further than anything else both in training your puppy and in showing in Junior Showmanship. Dogs must understand what is expected of them before they can do what you want, so it is essential that you know how to communicate with your dog in a calm, clear manner. You do not have to yell. A dog's hearing is a million times keener than yours. You do not have to manhandle the dog by pushing or pulling it around. Doing that will make your puppy hand shy. Once that happens you will have a hard time getting your dog to stand for you. You want to talk to your puppy in a firm but kind tone. The pup will not understand your words at first, but by *showing what* you want, your dog will learn what your expectations are.

Show and Obedience training are the same for young puppies. You can teach a dog to stand in one spot and stay on command, just as easily as you can teach it to sit in one spot. They are just different commands, which you will teach as separate exercises during your practice sessions.

Lessons

You and your puppy should spend a few minutes every day learning something new and practicing what you have learned the day before. Keep your learning sessions short and always end when the puppy has done something right. If you decide to follow the lessons taught in a particular book, read the book carefully beforehand, so that you will know exactly how to go about teaching the exercise to your dog. *Never work on one thing so long that the puppy gets tired or bored. If you find that you are becoming impatient, quit!* Never train a puppy or an adult dog when you are angry, upset or don't feel well. Dogs are very sensitive to your moods and they may think that you are upset with them. When that happens, you can forget about that lesson altogether.

Puppies learn in spurts, just as they grow in leaps and bounds. One week you may find that the puppy is responsive and happy to do whatever you ask. The next week it may do everything wrong, just as if you had never taught it that lesson. Don't despair. Take a few days off to walk around, play, throw a ball or just sit together and enjoy each other. When you return to the lessons, start from the beginning, as a refresher, just to make sure the puppy remembers what was taught before its brain went on vacation.

Never train a puppy vigorously when it is teething. You can walk your dog on a leash or do other simple things, but bear in mind that during this period the pup is not feeling well. The dog's teeth hurt and gums ache. A puppy may have diarrhea or run a slight fever. Sometimes its glands will swell and your dog may go off its food. The last thing that is needed is to be pulled by the neck and forced to do things it doesn't want to do. There will be plenty of

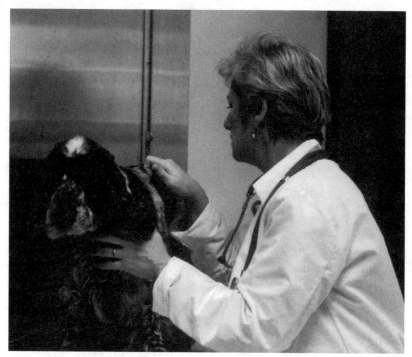

This veterinarian is giving an English Cocker Spaniel a general examination.

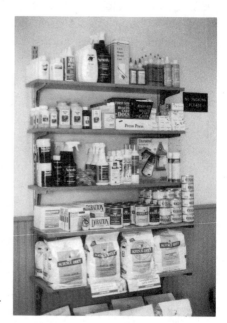

A display of health and nutrition products in a veterinarian's office.

time for lead breaking, stacking and gaiting once those difficult weeks are over.

Let your puppy enjoy puppyhood. They grow so fast that, before you know it, that cuddly ball of fur is eighty pounds of dog and the puppy antics are gone for good. Some of them you and your family are not going to miss! But the enthusiasm and energy that a puppy has should be treasured and nurtured, because those qualities are what make one dog a star and the other dog just average.

HEALTH

Your puppy's health is your responsibility. If you have purchased a healthy dog, keeping the dog that way depends on you. After you have brought your puppy home you should visit a veterinarian whom your family has selected. The veterinarian should examine the puppy for any signs of illness or defects which the breeder may not have mentioned. You should take a stool sample to the veterinarian so that it can be analyzed for *internal parasites*. If any are found, the puppy should be wormed promptly according to the veterinarian's instructions. Next to you, the veterinarian can be the most important person in your dog's life. That is why you should establish a good relationship early and maintain it throughout the dog's life with yearly check-ups and vaccinations.

Fleas and Ticks

From the beginning, your puppy should also be maintained free of *external parasites*, such as fleas and ticks. This is where regular grooming helps. You will notice rather quickly if these pests have been picked up when you go over your dog's skin and coat. If you notice that the puppy is scratching, biting or chewing on itself you can be sure that fleas are not far away. Nothing tears a coat faster than the destruction a dog does on itself to relieve the itching caused by fleas.

Flea control is not an easy task, but it must be done if you ever plan to have a presentable show dog, or even a comfortable pet. *Both the dog and the entire house must be treated in order to get rid of fleas.* Depending upon where you live, it is either a year-round task or a seasonal one. Even one flea bite can affect some dogs drastically if they have what is known as a flea allergy.

Ticks are dangerous because of the infections they carry, both to dogs and people. There are many species of ticks, some so small they are almost invisible, such as the deer tick. Others are easily seen as they attach themselves to the skin. These must be removed promptly and carefully, using a tweezers and alcohol to disinfect the area. The dog should be watched for any signs of illness following a tick bite.

There are flea and tick repellants which may be helpful in discouraging these pests from remaining on the dog, but all of them require that the dog be bitten in order for the repellant to kill the parasite. Still, in some areas of the country, it is better to take that chance than to do nothing.

GROOMING

Grooming involves more than running a brush over the surface of the coat, even if you have a short-haired breed. *Grooming involves keeping the nails trimmed, the ears clean and the coat washed and stripped of dead hair.*

Nail trimming is the most dreaded chore, usually because the puppy has had a bad experience. Once the clippers have cut into the quick of the nail, a dog never forgets. Some are more forgiving than others, but most will become very agitated and may even growl or snap. The best way to avoid these unpleasant encounters is to be extra careful at the beginning. When you first start to clip the nails, take off a small amount at the end of the nail, taking care not to cut into the quick where the blood supply and nerves make the nail sensitive. If your dog learns to trust you, it will be much easier later on. Always do the nails at the beginning of a grooming session, so that you get that unpleasantness over with. The dog will know that it will not be surprised at any moment to see the clippers come out if that chore is done initially.

If you are uncertain how to go about cutting the nails, ask someone with experience to demonstrate. Your veterinarian can do it, your breeder or fellow exhibitor. Do not fight with the dog over every nail. This is a time to calmly and firmly explain to the dog that you are the boss and this is going to be done, like it or not.

34

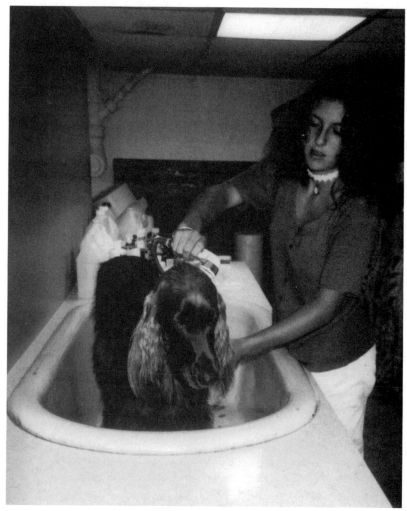

Always groom a *clean* dog. This Irish Setter is getting her weekly bath.

Some people wait until the dog is asleep on the couch to creep up and snip the nails. That may work, but at some point the dog will wake up and the fight begins all over. It's best to make it part of the grooming process and get it over with. Nails should be trimmed weekly or bi-weekly. Some dogs' nails seem to grow like weeds. Others grow slowly, so you can get away with fewer sessions. Cutting nails is not simply cosmetic, as nails that are too long can ruin a dog's feet and pasterns and affect the way a dog moves.

Ears should be cleaned weekly as part of the grooming process. If your dog has ears that are basically clean and healthy with

A veterinarian demonstrates the nail cutting procedure for the client to do at home.

little or no discharge you can use a cotton swab with plain alcohol to wipe out the ear canal. If the dog has been fussing, rubbing its head, scratching its ears and is exuding dark wax, a visit to the veterinarian is in order. The dog most likely is harboring a yeast infection or ear mites. Drop-eared dogs are particularly prone to ear problems because moisture accumulates in the ear canal, making an ideal climate for microorganisms to thrive.

You should be particularly attentive to the ears when you groom your dog. Sensitive ears translate to dogs who do not like to have their heads touched or collars tightened around the neck. This will make it more difficult for you to handle your dog in the show ring or even to take the dog for a walk.

Show Grooming

Every breed is groomed differently, depending on the fashion of the breed; the type of coat; length, color, amount of stripping, clipping and shaping required. You must take the time to learn from

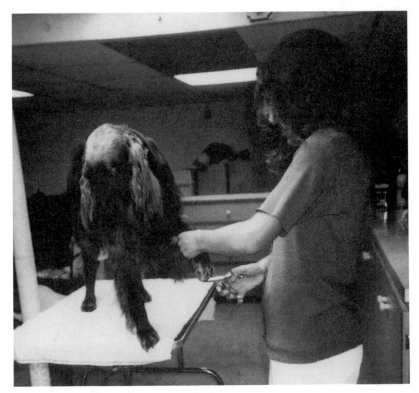
Nails are done first, so there are no surprises later.

an expert in your breed how to do the grooming properly. There is little sense in spending a lot of time learning to handle your dog correctly and then defeating yourself by neglecting the dog's appearance. Although Junior Showmanship judges are not supposed to evaluate the conformation quality of the exhibit, they will take into account whether you have prepared your dog well for the ring. No judge likes to go over a class full of dirty, unkempt animals, whether in the Junior classes or in the breed ring.

Show grooming takes time and should be done carefully and primarily at home. All the basics, such as nails, ears, bathing and trimming, should be done before you get to the show grounds. Once you are there you can brush, do a little extra trimming and generally spiff up your dog so that Star looks her absolute best just before you both go into the ring.

Grooming should be a pleasurable experience for you and your dog. If it is not, if the dog is constantly fighting and fidgeting, then you are doing something wrong. Grooming should be relaxing for

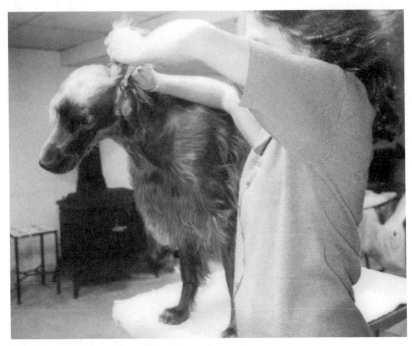

Ears should be cleaned weekly with a cotton swab.

the dog and an opportunity for you to become closer to the dog physically and emotionally. The secret to a happy relationship with a long-haired dog is to keep up with the hair. Once you have let the mats or knots accumulate so that every session becomes a tug-of-war, you will be frustrated and the dog will hate the process. A dog who hates to be groomed will associate that with the show ring, and you will have to work harder to make your canine partner enjoy the show experience.

Hair

There are different schools of thought about how to demat a dog in order to minimize damage to the coat. Cutting off the mats *doesn't* count! Dogs mat under the arms, under the tail and anywhere they are prone to scratch and chew because of the discomfort of fleas or allergies. Some dogs have the type of coat that seems to mat when you look at them, even though they are spotlessly clean and parasite-free. That is why it is so important to groom at least once a week and more often during shedding season.

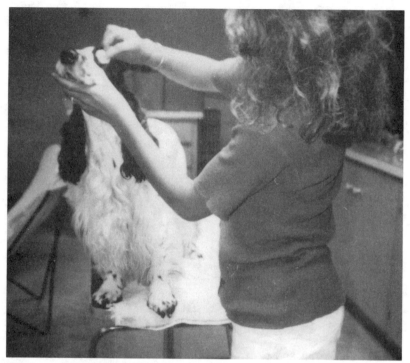
The eyes of this English Cocker Spaniel are wiped with a cotton swab.

If you have a double-coated dog, such as a Newfoundland, you will need a medium-tooth comb and a rake, which is a tool that looks like a small rake with a wooden handle. You can get through some of the dense coat and remove dead hair quite easily with the rake, but you must take care not to injure the skin. You will also need a pin brush, which is a brush with long, straight metal bristles. This is the main tool used to brush and maintain a double coat.

Here's where the difference is. Some people start at the head and work down the back to the tail and then down each side. Others work from the legs up to the center of the back on each side. Either way, lift the hair with one hand and brush down small amounts at a time until the whole coat has been brushed from the skin out to the ends of the hair. The other technique is to start at the ends of the hair and work back to the skin, using the same technique of holding the hair up with one hand and brushing with the other.

When you encounter a mat, you can either soften the mat with conditioner used full strength (not diluted with water) or a product such as No-More-Tangles. Then, with your fingers, work the solu-

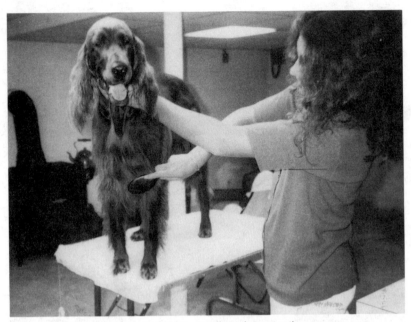

Hair and feathering are brushed down, small sections at a time.

tion into the mat and try to separate the hairs as much as possible before taking either a comb, rake or brush to the hair. Work the mat from the outside of the mat to the inside, gently pulling the hair apart at every stroke.

It is extremely helpful if the dog has been taught to lie quietly on its side on a grooming table while this procedure is going on. This lesson can be learned when the puppy is very small, when you first begin to brush it as part of its daily grooming routine. You should instruct the puppy to lie down, gently placing your dog on its side on the table and carefully brushing it for a few minutes, while you hold it still. Do not do this for more than five minutes at a time, first one side and then the other. This should be a calming experience for the puppy and one that it will come to enjoy. That way, when you get to do some serious grooming after the long coat starts to come in, the puppy will be accustomed to lying down on the table to be brushed. It will make it easier for you to reach every part of the body, especially the hard-to-reach places, such as under the arms and the stomach.

Short-haired dogs may not need the hours of brushing that the long-haired ones do, but that does not mean they should be neglected. They must be bathed weekly and their skin stimulated with

40

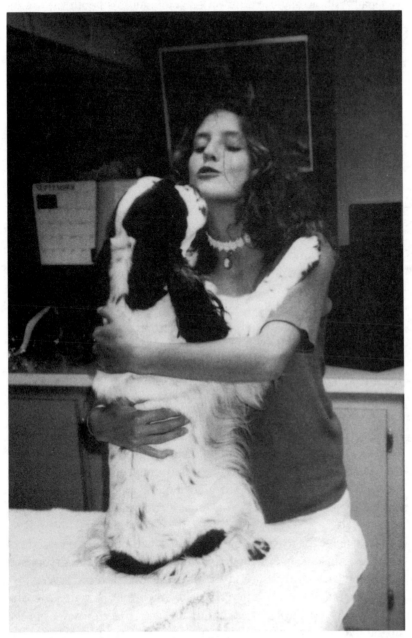

A big hug is a good reward when the session is over.

a good brushing with a soft bristle brush or a "hound glove." This is a pad with a rough texture on one side and a smooth texture on the other, and it is used to massage the skin and loosen any dead hair. Remember, nothing dies with the same coat of hair it's born with. Short-coated breeds shed, too, and you do not want judges to come away from examining your dog sporting a coat of hair which the dog has left on their clothing.

Grooming should always be done on a clean dog because brushing a dirty coat will break the hair. There are a million different shampoos and conditioners on the market. Find out what works for other people in your breed. Ask your breeder, mentor or friends what they use. Look to see which dogs look wonderful in the breed ring and try those products on your dog. You may find that some add that special shine and others do the opposite. Some dogs are allergic to the ingredients in some hair-care formulas and will sprout a coat of dandruff before your eyes, or will become red and itchy. Don't try a new regime just before an important show.

Short-haired dogs need only be rubbed dry with a towel. A couple of shakes and they are ready to go. Long-haired dogs can be left to dry on their own, or they must be blanketed in order to keep the hair lying smooth, or they must be dried under a blower. Setters and other long-coated breeds are usually wrapped in a blanket until the top coat dries. Other breeds, such as Old English Sheepdogs and dogs with coats that normally stand away from the body, are usually blow-dried. If you use a blower, do not use hot air, as this will dry out the coat. Use the blower on warm air only. Some dryers are equipped to blow only air, without heat of any sort. They will blow the water away from the coat but it is difficult to direct the flow of air with these air blasters. Different breeds require different techniques for blow drying, so you must learn what is appropriate for your breed.

Never, ever leave a dog in a crate with a blower on it. There have been instances in which dogs have been burned by dryers and have died of overexposure to the direct heat of a blow dryer.

Hair and coat condition are very important, but they depend very largely on the basic health of the dog. Hair grows from the inside out. A dog fed an optimum diet, that gets sufficient exercise to build up muscle and stamina, will grow a better and healthier coat than a couch potato that is a poor eater. All things work together to produce a happy, beautiful show dog.

4

The Anatomy of a Dog

THIS CHAPTER is not meant to intimidate anyone, nor is it a lesson in zoology. However, your dog is made up of the sum of its parts and it will help your show career if you know what those parts are and how they fit together. If you study the anatomy of your dog and then study your breed Standard you will know more than some of the judges standing in the middle of your ring.

Most dogs are built about the same. They have four legs, one in each corner, the same number of ribs (thirteen), one heart, two lungs, two ears, two eyes, one nose, one mouth, forty-two (give or take) adult teeth, one tail (long or short, natural or docked) and all of the various other components inside and outside of the skin which give each breed its individual characteristics.

As you stand around at ringside you will hear a lot of talk about "bend of stifle," "angulation," "slab-sided," "barrel-chested," "snipey" and many other references to different parts of the dog's anatomy. It will help you in showing your dog to its best advantage if you understand some of what makes a dog stand or gait the way it does. If you want to show off the dog's good hindquarters or forequarters, it helps to know where to put your hands or how to make the dog stand properly. If you want to show off the shoulders, you have to know where the shoulder blades come together at the withers.

Even more important, you should know what the good parts of your dog's anatomy are, and which parts to downplay as best you can. You can only know these things by understanding a little bit about anatomy and a lot about your breed.

THE HEAD

The head is made up of two main parts, the **muzzle** or **foreface** and the **skull**. These parts are connected in the middle by the bony portion of the head called the **stop**. Some breeds such as the Mastiff, St. Bernard or Pekingese have distinct, well-defined stops. Breeds such as the Collie, Saluki and Afghan Hound have almost no stop, as the muzzle gradually blends into the skull. In between these two extremes are all the other breeds with moderate or more or less pronounced stops.

Muzzles come in a great variety of lengths and widths. The Peke, with its distinct stop, has a very short, broad muzzle. The Collie has a long, tapered muzzle. In between is everything else.

The shape of the **skull** varies greatly, also. The Mastiff has a broad skull, the Saluki or Whippet an extremely narrow one. The total shape of the head and each of its parts is one of the most defining elements of the breeds and is a major characteristic of breed type.

Shape of the **eyes** from round to triangular to oval vary from breed to breed. The set of the **ears** into the skull, whether upright or dropped, is another defining characteristic. You have to know what is correct for your breed so that you can work with the eyes to get the proper expression and with the ears to achieve the overall desired look.

For instance, the Afghan Hound is supposed to have an aloof, faraway look. So you would not want to bait this dog so that it is focused right up close on your hand. The German Shepherd Dog, on the other hand, is supposed to be attentive and alert with a calm air of courage and intelligence. This dog is not supposed to be staring off into space or hanging around looking bored.

Whippets and Greyhounds are supposed to use their ears, so you will want to get their attention in front of the judge so that the

Three distinct head types are shown here. The English Setter has a moderately long, rectangular muzzle with a defined stop. The Afghan Hound has a long, narrow head with no stop. The Boxer has a short muzzle with a distinct stop.

ears come forward. When these breeds are in motion their ears lay back alongside the head. These are generally called rose ears.

Prick-eared breeds, such as the Norwich Terrier, the Akita or the Norwegian Elkhound, must keep their ears up. Some handlers put their finger and thumb behind the skull and push forward slightly behind the ears so the dogs' ears stay up and alert. Drop-eared dogs are not supposed to put their ears up, so they look as if they were coming out of the top of their heads. Setters, when excited, will lift

The Akita has pricked ears and an alert expression.

their ears, so instead of a soft, elegant expression they look comical. That's a difficult problem to overcome in a dog who has just spotted a squirrel or a bird flying by. Keeping the dog's attention on you will help, but sometimes nothing works, and you just have to let it focus on the bird. At least it will be doing what it was bred to do, and the judge may think you are clever to use that instinct.

The Bite

The dog's mouth is a sensitive part of the anatomy, and it is also one of the things every judge will focus on. There are three main types of mouths, usually called bites, although that is anatomically incorrect. There is the **overshot** mouth, in which the upper jaw comes out abnormally far over the lower jaw, so that the teeth do not fit together at all. This is a fault in every breed. There is the mouth in which the upper teeth fit tightly over the lower ones, so

The Shih Tzu has drop ears and an undershot mouth.

that the upper and lower *jaws* are about even in length. Most breeds consider this normal, and it is called a **scissors** bite. Another type is the **level** mouth, in which upper and lower jaws are exactly even so that the teeth meet in front. Many breed Standards consider this acceptable but not preferable to a scissors bite. Finally, there is the **undershot** mouth, in which the lower teeth protrude beyond the upper teeth due to the fact that the lower jaw is longer than the upper jaw. This is correct in breeds such as the Boxer and Lhasa Apso, and some other breeds of Asian origin.

How to Show the Mouth

When the judge asks you to show the bite, gently take your two fingers and lift the upper lip, holding on to the head or to the lead with your other hand. The judge wants to see whether the bite is correct for your breed. Some breed Standards call for the judge to count every tooth, because missing teeth are a disqualification. This is so in Golden Retrievers and Doberman Pinschers. In breeds

The exhibitor shows her Labrador Retriever's bite to the judge.

in which the whole dental structure must be examined, hold the dog's head in one hand and gently push the gum back away from the teeth on the side, so the judge can see the whole mouth. You may have to turn the head and do the same thing on the other side for those breeds.

A few breeds, such as the Chow Chow, must have black tongues and gums. You will have to open the dog's mouth gently so the judge can see. If you are clever about it you can train the dog to show an open mouth on command and save yourself a lot of fiddling in the ring. You can do this by offering a treat and giving it to the dog after it has opened its mouth on command. Do not fight with your dog over the bite. Use a gentle touch.

When the judge comes to the dog's head to look at the bite, do not shove the head at the judge. Let the judge approach the dog in a quiet manner. If you have a breed of dog which is judged on the table, place the dog at the edge of the table so that the judge

The judge examines the mouth of a Golden Retriever.

does not have to lean over the dog. This makes small dogs very apprehensive. You would not like to have some huge stranger bearing down on you, either.

FOREQUARTERS

After the judge has examined the bite and looked at the head, the next part of the body is the forequarters, consisting of the neck, forechest or prosternum, shoulder placement, withers and rib cage. You have to read your breed Standard to know what is called for in terms of shoulder angulation, forechest and length of neck. You can make a short-necked dog look as if it had a longer neck by pulling the head out and up, or you can make a long-necked dog look shorter by jamming the neck into the shoulders.

Shoulders

Many breeds call for "well-laid-back shoulders." This means that the angle of the **shoulder blade** (*scapula*) and the bone of the **upper leg** (*humerus*) meet at a rather pronounced angle at a joint called the point of the shoulder.

By positioning the dog's front legs well under the rib cage you can make the shoulder angle appear greater than it is. If the Standard calls for rather straight shoulder angulation you would place the front legs as far forward of the rib cage as possible. Bear in mind, however, that the dog will position itself in whatever way feels most comfortable. If your dog has pretty good shoulder angulation, leave it alone. Don't try to reconstruct nature, especially in the Junior Showmanship class, where the judge is supposed to be concentrating on how smoothly you show your dog. You do not want to be constantly fighting with your dog to try to reposition the limbs. Once you have set it up, leave it alone. If the front is not the dog's best feature, you do not want to call attention to it by constantly going back to fix something associated with it. You want to call the judge's attention to the best parts of your dog, not the worst.

You'll hear the term "loaded shoulders" sometimes. This means that the space between the shoulder blades at the top is wider than it should be, giving the dog a bulky appearance. Some

The judge examines the forequarters of this Akita, checking angulation.

breeds call for wide shoulders. Others call for shoulder blades that are close at the top. The top of the shoulder blades is called the **withers**. This is the point directly behind the neck where the shoulder blades come together. In most breeds, except for the Chesapeake Bay Retriever, the Old English Sheepdog and some of the Hound breeds, the withers is the highest point of the back. Many breeds call for the back to be level, which means that from the withers to the tail the back is the same height from the ground. Other breeds call for a moderate slope from withers to tail.

TOPLINE

The outline of the dog from the back of the skull to the tail is called the topline. Showing your dog so that the topline makes the

The judge feels for the spring of rib and body conformation on this Collie.

The Borzoi has a curved topline as called for in the Standard.

best picture you can is a very important part of Junior Showmanship. The topline is determined by the position of the head and neck, the placement of the shoulder blades, the strength of the back behind the withers, the set-on of the tail and the position of the rear legs, which influences the hindquarters.

The **back** of the dog is considered to be that part of the anatomy just behind the **withers** and in front of the **loin**. The back ends just about at the last rib. The loin begins where the back ends and extends to the hip bones where it blends into the **croup**. The croup is the area of the spine in back of the hips to where the buttocks end and the tail begins.

The entire topline is governed by the spinal cord, or vertebrae, which contains the central nervous system. Ribs, hips and shoulders are connected to the spinal cord by muscles and ligaments.

Some breeds have very distinctive toplines. The Greyhound, Whippet and Italian Greyhound present an outline which is completely different from most other breeds. They have a distinct arch over the loins which is caused by a curvature of the spine and a steeply sloping croup.

TAIL

The tail is a very important part of the topline and of the whole appearance of the dog. Most Standards are very specific about the tail. The set-on of the tail varies greatly from breed to breed and it, in turn, is governed by the way the croup is made. Some breeds specifically call for straight croups as part of the topline. Others, such as the English Cocker Spaniel, ask for a slightly rounded croup. Some breed Standards call for tails to be carried straight off the back. Others want tails curled over the back. Still others want them held up high. You have to know what is correct for your breed in order to show your dog correctly. Some breeds with docked tails, such as the English Springer Spaniel, call for tails to be carried slightly above the topline. Many handlers, however, push the tails up so they are carried high, which is incorrect. If you get a judge who knows the Standard for that breed, and you show your dog with the tail up in the air, you will be penalized. *You have to know your Standard and how it relates to the anatomy of your dog.*

HINDQUARTERS

Finally, the hindquarters. The hindquarters propel the dog forward. That is what they do, besides, of course, allowing the dog to stand up on all fours! Hindquarters vary greatly among the breeds. The extremes are the German Shepherd Dog with the long, sweeping thigh and short rear pasterns, contrasted with the Chow Chow or the Chinese Shar-Pei, which has almost straight hindquarters. One is very angulated, the other has very little angulation. The angulation comes from the position of the pelvic bones and the upper and lower leg bones, which are joined at the stifle joint.

In setting up your dog, the hock (rear pastern) should always be perpendicular to the ground. If you stretch the rear leg so that the rear pastern is slanted backwards, the dog will lose angulation because those joints will be stretched out. If the rear legs are set under the dog, the topline will look as if the croup is higher than the back. Even in breeds such as the Borzoi, which has a rounded topline because of the configuration of the spinal column, the rear pasterns should be perpendicular to the ground.

One of the most common faults affecting the hindquarters of almost any breed is cowhocks. Cowhocks occur when the hock joints bend inward toward one another. In most breeds cowhocks are a fault. You can set your dog up so that it appears that the hocks are straight, but if the dog moves, the hocks will come together again. If you have a dog with this fault try to set it up correctly and then keep the dog standing without moving. You do not want to be constantly paying attention to the rear. Each time you are asked to move the dog, as you go up the line toward the front, you will have to set your dog up again. Do it once and then do not look back. Remember, you want to call attention to the best parts of your dog's anatomy, not the faults.

The judge goes to the rear of this Golden Retriever to examine the hindquarters and stance of the dog.

BALANCE

The most important thing to remember in making a picture of your dog is that the front and the rear should be balanced. As far as possible, the angles of the shoulder and those of the hip should be about the same. If your dog is made properly that is easy to do. That kind of dog will set itself up and look good, no matter what you do. If your dog has faults, and most of them do, in either the

This Junior makes a picture of confidence with his Afghan Hound.

front or rear angulation, you have to try to compensate for that by the way you handle it. You have to practice in front of a mirror to see what picture you are making. Then you should have someone who knows what they are looking at evaluate your performance.

Knowing a little of the basic anatomy of how your dog is put together will make it easier for you to understand why it moves and stands the way it does.

Understanding anatomy can also be helpful if your dog comes up lame. You will be able to describe to the veterinarian what you are seeing. You might be able to pinpoint where the trouble is if you know how to feel the bones and know where the joints are. That is a big part of the diagnosis, and because you are with the dog more than the veterinarian, your observation can be very helpful in determining what is wrong and what needs to be done about it.

Anatomy involves not only the skeleton, which we have been talking about in this chapter, but all the other internal systems of the dog—circulatory, digestive, respiratory, nervous and endocrine systems. While they are all essential to the health and well-being of your dog, you cannot influence them directly.

SKIN—THE BODY'S LARGEST ORGAN

Everything within the dog is encased in the skin. You can consider skin something like a suitcase into which you put all your stuff to carry around. You zip it up and everything stays inside. The same principle is true for the skin, yours as well as your dog's. The skin is a mirror of the health of your dog, too. If the skin is healthy and the coat, which grows out of the skin, is shiny and glowing, then you know your dog is in good health. The skin is an anatomical barometer of the health of your dog, and as such, it is important for you to observe it carefully on a regular basis. It can tell you more than almost anything else whether your dog is feeling well inside.

TYPE

Finally, there is that almost indefinable thing called type. Type is what makes one breed distinct from another. *Without breed type, all dogs would be mutts.* Although there is nothing wrong with nice dogs of indeterminate origins, since they are made up of different breeds, they are never the same. Type is the sum of all the parts of a dog's anatomy from the head to the tail. Type distinguishes one breed from another and it also distinguishes dogs within a breed.

Sometimes you will hear about different types within a breed. This usually refers to certain characteristics of the head and expression or of body style. In many cases, one type is correct and the others are wrong, but breeders tend to support their own lines by claiming that more than one type is acceptable. Within most breeds there is an honest difference of opinion regarding type, and you have to study your breed thoroughly to understand type and how it is conveyed through anatomy. The way the dog is built will determine whether it is typical for its breed.

You can now see that anatomy has a real bearing on competition and showmanship, so it is worth your while to study a little about it.

5

When to Call
the Veterinarian

T HE HEALTH AND WELL-BEING of your dog should be the first priority in your relationship. Dog shows should be fun for the dog as well as for you, and a dog that is not feeling well will not show well. What is more important, however, is the fact that the health of your dog is the responsibility of you and your family.

Dogs cannot tell you when they are not feeling well, but there are other ways in which they may communicate how they feel. You must be observant to the signals your dog sends you. You and your family must be aware of changes in behavior or attitude and alert to physical symptoms.

Dogs that are being shown and are therefore exposed to many other animals are more likely to pick up diseases than those that never leave the backyard. Dogs on the show circuits should be current on all their vaccinations. Many veterinarians suggest that parvovirus boosters be given twice a year to those dogs rather than the annual vaccinations which all dogs should have. In addition, boosters for kennel cough and other respiratory illnesses are useful for those who are exposed to a great number and variety of dogs. It is important for dogs in contact with other dogs to be checked for mycoplasma and brucellosis, and genital diseases, which may cause infertility or aborted fetuses.

INTESTINAL DISEASES

The easiest symptoms of disease to spot are those signaling intestinal problems. Dogs that have diarrhea or are vomiting are clearly unwell. There are many causes for intestinal disease. Parvovirus or coronavirus are fairly common, especially in puppies or young dogs. Diarrhea and vomiting should be considered medical emergencies in puppies, because they can become dehydrated very quickly. If your puppy shows these symptoms and does not recover by itself within twelve hours, you should take it to a veterinarian.

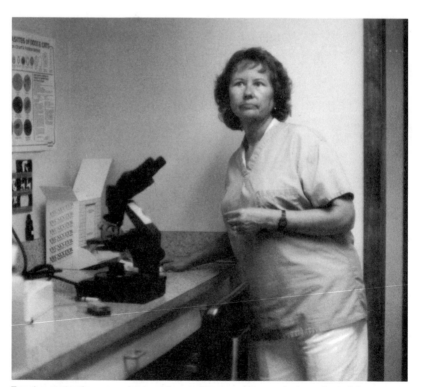

Fecal examinations are done under a microscope by a veterinary technician.

Puppies, and even many older dogs, put everything within range into their mouths, so eating inappropriate stuff is often a cause of an intestinal upset. Many times this resolves itself, but if you suspect your dog may have gotten into some poisonous material, such as insecticides, household cleaners, poisonous plants (of which there are many) or pest-control products, that, too, requires immediate medical attention.

EARS

When you groom or bathe your dog, there are a few things which should be part of general hygiene. We mentioned care of the ears, especially for long-eared breeds. Ears should be cleaned with plain alcohol or a mixture of alcohol and water on a piece of cotton once weekly. Dark exudate (material in the ear) indicates either a yeast infection or the presence of ear mites. These conditions need to be treated promptly. They are often recurring problems, so you need to be attentive to them constantly. Some dogs are more prone to developing ear problems than others. Often this has to do with the configuration of the ear canal.

EYES

The eyes are another part of the examination you should do on your dog. If they tear excessively or if they are producing yellow discharge (or any discharge) there is something wrong. Some breeds, such as the Pekingese and others with large and protruding eyes, are exceptionally prone to eye diseases and these breeds must be carefully watched.

Any dog can get an eye injury from running through tall grass or getting grass seeds or debris under the protective third eyelid. Sometimes these foreign bodies must be removed by a veterinarian with the dog under light anesthesia. Often, however, bathing the eye with a boric acid solution is enough to dislodge stuff that has gotten into the eyes during the normal course of play or exercise.

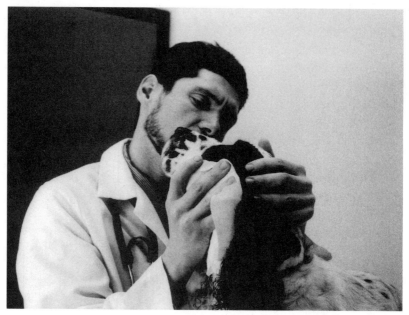
A veterinarian examines the eyes of an English Cocker Spaniel to check for entropion and other eye problems.

ALLERGIES

Some dogs have allergies which may manifest themselves by red, runny eyes, just as people do. These may be treated topically by applying drops or salve to the eyes, under the direction of a veterinarian. This may be enough if the eyes are the only part affected, but seasonal or other allergy symptoms usually involve other parts of the body as well.

Allergies are one of the most difficult, and yet most common, sources of skin disease, irritation, itching, scratching and general discomfort to the dog. Skin allergies usually begin to show up by the time the dog is two years old. They may be seasonal, in response to the bloom of various plants or molds, or they may be year-round problems, which would indicate something in the environment which is present all the time. Examples might be carpet fibers, dust and cleaning products.

Whatever people are allergic to can also affect dogs. Owners can spend a great deal of money trying to find out what the dog is allergic to and then treating it. Unless the condition is cleared up, however, you will have an uncomfortable dog that will be unhappy with itself and will never be in condition to be shown.

Food allergies are a plague for many dogs. Once these are identified and the offending food replaced, these allergies are usually resolved satisfactorily, although it may take some time to figure out what ingredients the dog is allergic to. Sometimes sensitivity tests (''scratch tests'') are performed on dogs, just as they are on people. In some cases, natural or home-cooked foods may be recommended. Your veterinarian may elect to refer the dog to a veterinary dermatologist or allergist to diagnose and treat the dog in the most appropriate manner.

ANAL GLANDS

During your dog's weekly examination and bathing you should pay attention to the anal glands. These are small glands located on either side of the anal opening. They secrete a rather smelly substance when the dog marks its territory, which is undetectable to humans. These glands sometimes become full and uncomfortable for the dog. You can see this if the dog licks itself or scoots along the floor on its bottom. Doing this does not usually indicate the presence of worms; it often is a symptom of anal glands which must be expressed. Your veterinarian can do this, and can also show you or your parent how to do this in the bathtub. If left untreated, anal glands can become infected; they are then a much more difficult and expensive problem to treat. Infected anal glands can also, for some unknown reason, cause the ears to become inflamed, and often when the ears are red and itchy the anal glands are involved.

PARASITES

Dogs who are being shown should be checked for internal parasites *at least* twice a year. The most common intestinal worms are **roundworms**, **hookworms** and **whipworms**. **Tapeworms** are also fairly common but are the most benign of these parasites.

Round, hook and whip are found in the soil, are easily transmitted and can be carried from dam to puppies through the placenta. These parasites are detected by taking fecal samples to your vet, who then examines them under a microscope. Roundworms are common in puppies, but a heavy infestation can cause anemia and even death. Hookworms and whipworms are often the cause of a dog looking poorly. These parasites affect the dog internally, will cause dry haircoat, anemia, unthriftiness, diarrhea or bloody stools. There are specific worming products which should be obtained through your veterinarian to treat all these problems. Tapeworms are transmitted through fleas or rabbits (depending upon the variety of tapeworm) and are rather easily eliminated from the intestinal tract.

Many show kennels either worm their dogs monthly or, at the least, do monthly fecal checks on all the dogs in the kennel. You should do this with your show dogs at home. It is one of the ways you can ensure that your dog is in optimum health.

Heartworm is another parasite which is carried by many varieties of mosquitoes and is found everywhere that mosquitoes are. Heartworms mature in the bloodstream and the adult worms lodge in the heart, affecting the arteries and lungs. There are preventatives on the market which should be given to all dogs at risk of exposure to this parasite. Dogs should be tested twice a year for heartworm, even those already on the preventative. Veterinarians will not prescribe heartworm medication without test results showing that no evidence of heartworm is present.

A fairly recent parasite, which is really a bacterium, is the one which causes **Lyme disease**. Lyme disease is carried by several varieties of ticks. The bacterium is carried through the bloodstream and may lodge in any part of the body. It may cause lameness, pain in the joints and many other symptoms, depending upon where it stays in the body. Lyme disease in dogs often causes fever, lethargy, lack of appetite and pain. If left untreated, it may cause other problems later on, from kidney disease to neurological diseases.

Ticks also carry other unpleasant illnesses, among them Rocky Mountain spotted fever and Erlichiosis.

During the season when ticks are active, dogs should be checked every day, the ticks removed with a tweezers and the site of the bite cleaned with alcohol or other disinfectant. Lyme disease is not found in every part of the country, but the range of its habitat

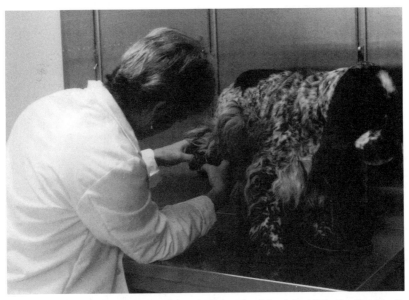

An English Cocker Spaniel is having a foot examined to determine why the dog is limping. This could be a symptom of Lyme disease.

seems to be spreading farther every year. It is a major source of illness in people as well as in dogs. Both are treated with the same antibiotics over a protracted length of time.

GENETIC DISEASES

There are some genetic diseases which afflict dogs. If you own a breed which is known for them you should be aware of this, so that you will know if your dog shows any of the signs. It would be impossible to list them all in this book, but there are books in the AKC library which list the genetic diseases common in various breeds. In addition, your veterinarian can find out for you whether your breed is known to produce certain illnesses or conditions. For instance, many breeds are prone to various types of skin diseases. In addition, there are genetic eye problems, kidney and liver diseases and endocrine diseases which occur in various breeds.

Although your breeder should be honest and knowledgeable enough to tell you about them, this does not always happen. If you study up on your breed, you will be able to find out whether your

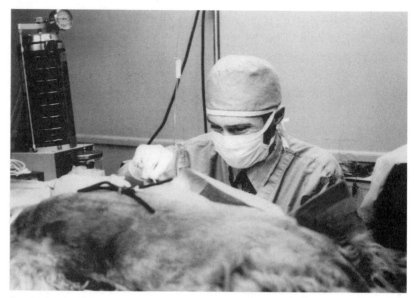

Surgical procedures such as spaying and neutering safeguard a dog's health and prevent unplanned breedings.

dog may be affected, and you will then know what to look for if any of the symptoms occur. It is not a pleasant prospect, but good owners should be knowledgeable about their dogs. Your family, along with your veterinarian and your breeder, should be able to assist you in doing this research.

HEATSTROKE

Finally, anyone who goes to a show when the weather is hot should be aware of the possibility that dogs are at risk of dying of heatstroke. Dogs need ventilation. They need to be kept in an area which is shaded or in a building with good air flow. Dogs need to be attended. Many times owners park a vehicle in the shade and leave, forgetting that the earth moves, so the position of the sun moves, and what was in shade in the morning is in the sun in the afternoon. Too often, at dog shows, owners are more interested in gabbing at ringside than attending to their responsibilities.

When the weather is hot, a dog taken out of an air-conditioned van or motor home and run around in the hot sun will go down with heatstroke sooner than the dog who has been acclimated to being in the heat. People can shed their jackets and ties. Dogs cannot shed their fur coats. Dogs sweat through their mouths and the pads of their feet. While they are panting they are producing volumes of hot air, heating up the air around them. Several dogs in a car will heat up the air in a matter of minutes. Even one dog, left in a vehicle without adequate air flow, can overheat in a very short time. It is absolutely the responsibility of the owners to keep their dogs cool and comfortable. Sometimes, owners will leave a dog in a motor home or van with a generator running the air-conditioning. Terrible accidents have occurred when the generators failed and the dogs died because no one was in attendance.

Symptoms of heatstroke are excessive panting, drooling, weakness, collapse, vomiting and diarrhea, elevated temperature, seizures and death. Dogs that appear to be hot, but not in dire straits, can be treated by immersion in cool, not freezing, water and removed to a cool or air-conditioned place. Alcohol placed on the pads of the feet and in the groin will assist in cooling because it will evaporate quickly and feel cold to the skin. Dogs that are obviously in serious distress should be rushed to the nearest veterinarian. They will need to be cooled with enemas and given intravenous fluids until their temperature comes down.

Dogs that survive heatstroke must be carefully watched over several days because stress of any kind can send the temperature up and the heart into distress.

Preventative Measures

Always carry a jug of water and water the dog frequently throughout the day at shows. Ice is not the best thing to give dogs. They are better off with cool water. Soaking the feet in water will also help to keep the dogs cool. Remember that black dogs absorb the heat and will overheat in the sun faster than light-colored dogs, whose coats will reflect the heat to some degree. If you are standing ringside, find the shade or the tent. Do not keep your dog out in the hot sun. This may seem obvious, but stand at a show on any day in the summer and see how many people, adults as well as children, are gabbing away as their dogs are panting at their sides.

Heatstroke is always a medical emergency. It is preventable and inexcusable.

BLOAT

Although this is not a book on medical emergencies, there is *one life-threatening illness which every owner, adult and child, should be able to recognize* if you own a breed which is predisposed to bloat.

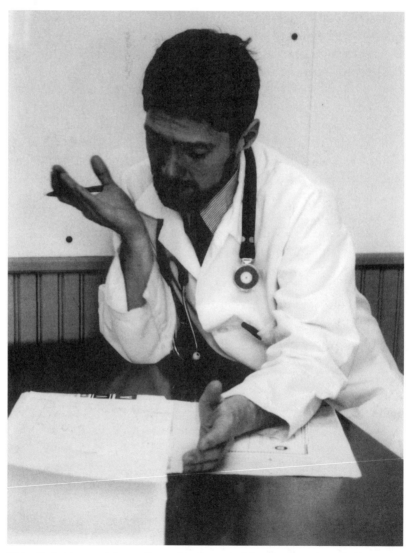

The veterinarian explains a diagnosis after examining the records and history of a patient.

Bloat is a condition in which the stomach fills with air, cutting off passage of food into the intestines and preventing air or food from being eliminated by vomiting. The stomach fills with gas and sometimes twists in the abdominal cavity, cutting off the blood supply. This is called torsion.

A dog may bloat with or without torsion. Large, deep-chested breeds, such as St. Bernards, Great Danes, Bloodhounds, Irish Setters and German Shepherd Dogs are prone to bloat. Symptoms are pacing, restlessness and inability to defecate or vomit, although the dogs will try to do this. The abdomen will feel tight and will resound like a drum when it is lightly tapped. In the early stages of bloat the abdomen may not expand dramatically, so that is not a good indication of the presence of bloat.

Bloat is always a medical emergency and must be treated by a veterinarian promptly if the dog is to be saved from death.

Conditions such as bloat, heatstroke and many other illnesses which dogs may get are treatable if they are caught in time. That is why it is so important for owners to be alert to any changes in their dogs' physical condition or behavior. It is all part of being responsible.

The judge gives instructions about where she wants the dog to be gaited and in what pattern.

6

Interpreting the Rules

ALL AMERICAN KENNEL CLUB events are governed by a set of rules, regulations and guidelines. The regulations concerning who may exhibit and what show-giving clubs must do and guidelines for judges and for Junior exhibitors are set down in a small booklet available from AKC at no charge to anyone who asks.

The booklet describes who may enter Junior Showmanship and the stipulation that the dog entered in this class must be owned by the Junior or a member of the Junior's family or household. Bitches in season may not be shown in Junior competition, but substitution may be made if specified procedure is followed.

Children from age ten up to their eighteenth birthday may compete in Junior Showmanship. There are classes for Novice Juniors and Open Juniors. Juniors may show in the Novice class until they have three first placements in that class with competition, after which they must move up to Open. Clubs may elect to divide both sections by age groups, Novice Junior and Open Junior are for children between the ages of ten and fourteen. (Match shows may allow children eight years and older to compete.) Open Junior and Open Senior are for children ages fourteen to eighteen.

Clubs may also offer a class for Best Junior Handler in which the winners from the previous classes compete for the top award. One may think that the Best Junior is automatically won by the oldest and most experienced handler, but that is not always the case. The Best Junior may come out of any of the classes, depending upon the competition on the day and the ability of the handler to present his or her dog to best advantage.

The central theme of the rules and guidelines is contained in this sentence: "Junior Showmanship shall be judged solely on the ability and skill of the Juniors in handling their dogs as in the breed ring."

The conformation quality of the dog is not considered here, but the catch is that persons who elect to judge Junior Showmanship

Judge explains to the class before she begins her examinations what will be done. She does this to make the Juniors feel more at ease and confident.

must have a working knowledge of how each breed is supposed to be presented. It is incumbent upon Junior Showmanship judges to do their homework, to watch every breed that will be shown before them on a particular day so that they can properly evaluate whether the Juniors are doing their jobs satisfactorily. Lists of dogs entered at shows in Junior classes are available from the Superintendents beforehand and should be sent to the Junior judge for that particular day. Of course, more thorough preparation would indicate that judges would have spent considerable time watching all of the breeds before applying to judge Junior Showmanship, but that does not appear to happen all the time.

The purpose of Junior Showmanship classes is contained in another important section of the guidelines. It states that:

> "The purpose of Junior Showmanship Competition is twofold: to introduce and encourage Juniors to participate in the sport of dogs; and to provide Juniors with a meaningful competition in which they can learn, practice and improve in all areas of handling skill and sportsmanship."

THE JUDGES' ROLE

Both the judge and the Junior have important contributions to make to fulfill the stated purpose. Judges are expected to have a real interest in Juniors and in the concepts guiding the competition. Judges should teach by example. The guidelines state that they should be "prompt, courteous, patient and properly attired." They must show no bias to any child or to or against any breed of dog.

It is also the judge's responsibility to be concerned with safety in the ring and to organize the class so that no child or dog is at risk. If a child comes into the ring with an obviously unmanageable dog, it is up to the judge to ask that child to leave for his/her own safety and that of others in the class. Any dog showing signs of viciousness must be excused immediately. The judge is in complete command of the activities in any ring, and under circumstances of safety, or of opinion as to who is to be awarded the ribbons on that day, the judge has the final say. A judge's ruling is seldom open to dispute, even though it may be disappointing to the Juniors who are left out of the ribbons.

She indicates where the first person in line is to stand. The others will follow behind.

Judges are required to use the usual gaiting patterns which are commonly seen in the breed rings. They are required to treat all entrants the same, allotting about the same amount of time to each exhibitor, until competition is narrowed to a small group of finalists. Judges do not have to spend a lot of time evaluating the dogs, because, remember, it is the handler being judged in this class. Enough time should be allowed, however, so that each Junior can show the dog to best advantage.

Judges should not confuse Juniors with unnecessary movements or unclear instructions. Judges must make themselves understood by word and gesture so that Juniors do not have to try to interpret some gobbledygook or sign language. This situation, unfor-

The judge approaches an exhibitor who is holding her Borzoi's head with one hand and the lead in the other.

tunately, is seen fairly often in the breed ring, and there is no excuse for it there, either.

The guidelines for judges state that they should evaluate the Juniors in four basic areas: proper breed presentation, skill in the individual dog's presentation, knowledge of ring procedures and appearance and conduct. The judge should reward the handler whose technique shows the greatest economy of motion. Judges are asked to fault Juniors who use exaggerated motions and gestures when showing their dogs.

Judges are asked to find those Juniors who possess a "hand for dogs." In essence, this means handlers who neither over- nor underhandle their dogs. To do this the judge must look both at the handler and the dog. Is the dog responsive to the handler? Do they work as a team? Does the dog appear posed or interested at all times? Is the dog under control? Is the dog gaited correctly? Are the

She shows the bite to the judge.

dog's main faults being minimized, or conversely, are its virtues accentuated? Are dog and handler relaxed?

Judges will have little difficulty in determining which Juniors have a good knowledge of ring procedures. Do they follow instructions? Are they at ease when asked to do something different?

The judge must also take into account whether the Junior is dressed appropriately. Whether the dog is trimmed and groomed according to the style of the breed and the overall conditioning of the dog (to have been done by the Junior) are evaluated as well. A Junior's general conduct in the ring will play a big part in the judge's decision. Unsportsmanlike conduct or actions and Juniors who are heavy-handed or impatient with their dogs should be penalized.

All of the above is seen from the judge's point of view. Juniors have the responsibility of presenting their dogs in the best possible way.

This Junior is free-baiting her Borzoi, showing an economy of movement.

THE JUNIORS' ROLE

Junior Showmanship classes are held so that young people can:

- Experience winning and losing among those who are similar in age.
- Learn the correct way to handle the breed they own.
- Practice handling skills in competition.
- Prepare for handling their dog in the regular classes.

Classes are organized so that Juniors will be asked to move their dogs with the rest of the class, to present the dog in the standing position proper for the breed, including the use of a table for those

The Junior gaits her dog across the ring . . .

breeds normally examined in that way, and to move the dog individually in a regular pattern.

When moving or standing with the rest of the class, Juniors should not crowd the dog and handler in front of them and must be able to control their dogs at all times. Sometimes one sees a very

and returns to the judge on the diagonal.

small child attempting to pilot a very large dog, one that the young-ster cannot control should the dog decide to leave the ring or pounce on another dog. Children should not be encouraged to enter Junior Showmanship classes with animals inappropriate to the spirit of the class.

Juniors should be neat, clean and well groomed. Clothing and jewelry should not distract, limit or hinder the judge's view of the dog. Dogs should be clean and properly groomed for the breed. They should strive to make the dog stand out as the most important part of the team of dog and handler.

In handling their dogs *understatement is desirable*. Juniors should keep the dog's attention without using dramatic or superflu-ous hand movements. They should gait their dogs in a controlled trot, always keeping the dog in view of the judge. Juniors should concentrate on their dog and not on the judge, and they should never use exaggerated posture, motions or gestures which call attention to themselves instead of the dog.

Many of the rules by which Juniors are judged and which Juniors must learn in order to compete successfully are applicable to many other facets of life. Poise, self-assurance, personal hygiene and appearance, the ability to control oneself and one's surroundings and athleticism all play a part in show handling.

She presents the dog to the judge on her return.

Small dogs are gaited together at the end of the line when there are several large dogs in the class.

Many of the most successful Juniors, some of whom went on to careers as professional handlers or breeders/exhibitors, had interests in fields other than dog shows. They were horseback riders, soccer players, musicians, honor students, heads of the student council. They used their talents in the show ring to foster their abilities in many disciplines. Conversely, their physical endurance and intellectual curiosity made them better in Junior Showmanship competition. They were able to use their abilities of leadership and teamwork to communicate with their dogs with sensitivity and with greater ease than children who did not develop those skills. The most successful juniors are those who are able to analyze themselves and their dogs in order to improve and perfect their mutual performances.

Knowing what is expected and how to achieve it are separate things. In the following chapters we will try to show you how your goal of being the best Junior Handler may be attained.

7

Learning the Basics

THERE ARE REALLY only two basic components to showing a dog. Everything else is icing on the cake. These two essentials are stacking and gaiting. That's easy, you say? Well . . . no it isn't. It requires a lot of patience, coordination and teamwork between you and your dog.

STACKING

It is important to teach your dog one thing at a time. First you teach the dog to stack—that is, to stand in one spot with all four feet facing in the same direction without wiggling and doing the two-step with its legs. Dogs have the most amazing ability to turn themselves into pretzels or jelly whenever they are asked to stand up. But just show them a cookie and they are on full alert! You can *use this enthusiasm* to get your dog to stand perfectly, but first you should be able to control the dog by using your hands.

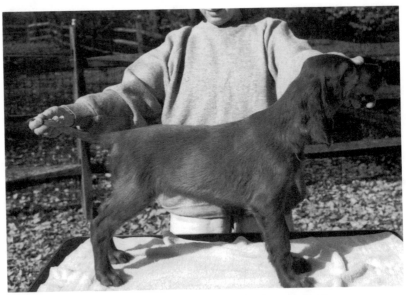
Teaching a young Irish Setter puppy to stack can begin on the table.

Look Before You Stack

Before you attempt to do this yourself, have a friend or your parent stack the dog for you so you can see what it looks like from the judge's point of view. Stand back, notice where the front legs are placed, where the hind legs are placed and what happens to the dog's head at one end, tail at the other and body in between. Most breeds, no matter how big or how small, are stacked in the same way. Front legs are positioned with feet facing forward, shoulders and elbows on about the same line. Rear legs are placed with hocks perpendicular to the ground. If you look at pictures of your breed, and you observe dogs in the conformation ring, you will get a good idea of how your dog should look when it is posed (stacked) in show position.

Your Turn

Once you see how your dog looks with someone else holding it, try to do it yourself. You may find that you have to adjust your own position from kneeling to standing, depending upon the size of

Teaching an English Cocker Spaniel to stack is also done on the ground.

the dog compared to the length of your arms. One of the problems Juniors have, especially younger ones, is that they are unable to stack a dog in its usual position for the breed because they are just not tall enough. We are not suggesting that you go out and buy a small dog, although as we mentioned in the last chapter, any Junior who cannot control his or her dog will be asked to leave the ring.

You will have to find a way to get the dog to stand still, looking good and not like a figure eight, that is comfortable for you. *You probably will have to train the dog to stand still.* That takes more time and work than wrestling it into position, but when you have achieved that goal you will be able to make a very impressive

When this Junior stacks her Samoyed she looks to see if the dog's feet are positioned properly.

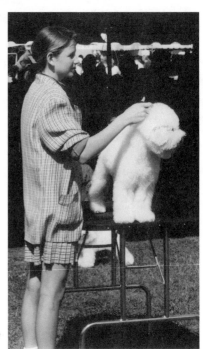

Stacking a Bichon Frisé on the table to be ready for the judge.

statement in the show ring. Training will also allow you to stack your dog in a very short time so that when the judge comes down the line you will be ready. *You should eventually be able to stack a dog in about thirty seconds.* When you consider that the judge has only two minutes to examine a dog, you don't want to waste time fidgeting while the judge is waiting for you.

Training lessons should be short. You do not want the dog to become restless or bored or you will be defeated before you ever step inside the baby gates that make up most show rings. Ten minutes morning and evening should be all you spend on teaching your dog to stack.

There are two types of stacking positions, the hard stack and the free-bait. When you do a hard stack you hold the dog's head and tail while you either stand or kneel alongside or behind with the dog between you and the judge. Cardinal Rule: **ALWAYS POSITION THE DOG BETWEEN YOU AND THE JUDGE!** Once you have the dog positioned, and it looks correct, praise the dog and release. Don't keep the stack for more than a minute or two at the beginning, because the dog will certainly start to fidget and you will lose control.

Economy—the Key to Success

Don't move feet more than is necessary (the dog's, that is). If your dog's front feet are set up right and only the back feet need fixing, then just move the foot that needs correcting. If the back feet are okay and one front foot turns out or in, fix just that one foot. In other words, the less fussing you have to do the easier and quicker it will be to set your dog up properly. Remember, the judges' guidelines call for economy of motion.

Juniors lose more classes by fussing with their dogs on the stack than anything else. You don't want to be fiddling with your dog when everyone else is already in position. Hard stacking is much more difficult than free-baiting, but it is a good thing to learn for any breed. There may be times that your dog just isn't interested in food or squeaky toys, and you will wish you learned how to set the dog up using both methods.

Stacking—Step by Step

When you go to set the legs where you want them, *grasp the leg at the elbow, never at the ankle*. Where possible, lean over the dog to set the leg on the outside. Naturally, if you have a giant breed, you will have to reach underneath and try to position the leg.

Stacking a long-haired Dachshund on the ground is difficult outdoors.

At no time should you let go of the head while you are fixing the rear or the legs. You must always keep control of the dog, either with the lead clutched in your hand, or with your hand underneath the chin. If you allow the dog's head to droop, it will look awful, and more important, you lose complete control, so that the dog can just walk away anytime it feels like it.

If you have a large breed in which it is almost impossible to get around or under the dog without losing control, you will have to walk it into a stack—that is, leave enough room in front of you so that the dog can take a few steps forward as you look to see whether all the legs are positioned properly. Once you see that they are placed underneath the dog so that the animal looks good, Stop! A dog that has been trained to stand on command should be able to hold that position without moving, while you either stand by the head or kneel alongside or behind your dog, whichever custom your breed calls for.

FREE-BAITING

Breeds that are free-baited require that you learn how to properly position your dog using a reward such as liver, hot dogs, toys or tennis balls to get the animal's attention. Dogs such as Collies, Shelties and Dobermans customarily are free-baited, although almost any breed can be taught to free-bait. The purpose is to get the dog to stand four-square on its own feet, in proper position, with the head up and looking alert, eyes on you. Free-baiting works best with a dog with no major structural faults. If you have a dog, however, with a terrible rear or a terrible front and you free-bait it, that fault will be most obvious to the judge, unless you train the dog to correct its own stance. Remember, one of the things the judge is looking for is how the handler minimizes faults or maximizes good points.

When you use a treat to get the dog's attention, be sure that you keep it in full view so that the dog's head and neck are positioned correctly. *Don't* use your arm as a windmill, moving the bait up and down in all directions. This is not an eye exam. You want the dog to stand steady, looking at you and staying in one position. If you free-bait you will have to teach the dog by word and motion how to

This Junior free-baits her Dachshund to show expression.

correct itself if the feet are going in different directions. When you practice, you will have to position the feet properly and then reward the dog for standing still.

After each lesson, give a lot of praise, and just a tiny morsel of the treat you are using. Too many handlers, both Juniors and others, litter entire rings with bait so that dogs go down and back with their noses on the ground, grazing along instead of gaiting

These two Juniors are free-baiting their dogs, a Miniature Pinscher and a Smooth Fox Terrier, as the judge goes down the line to see the picture made by each team.

properly. Dropping goodies in the ring is inconsiderate to fellow exhibitors. If you happen to drop something by mistake, be sure you pick it up before you leave the ring.

A lot of posturing and artificial motions go on in rings where dogs are free-baited. Keep your hands quiet and use as few motions as possible to attract and keep your dog's attention.

This brings up an important point. Always have a reason for doing something. Don't just copy someone else, even if that person is the most successful handler in your breed. Just because he or she does something with a particular dog does not mean it will look good on you or be right for your dog. Try to *figure out why* that handler is doing something with the lead or with bait or with hands to enhance the dog's appearance. What is it about the handler's dog that requires that particular handling move? It might be appropriate for that particular dog, but not for yours. You must always try to handle your dog in the way that looks best. And that is not necessarily the way another dog would look good.

Free-baiting practice should take no more time than hard stacking, five or ten minutes twice a day. Longer than that will bore you and the dog.

USING THE LEAD

Another component to your stacking practice is use of the lead. There are hundreds of different types of show leads. Choose the one that is the easiest for you to use and that gives you the most control. Choose a lead that fits your dog. You would not put a half-inch-wide choke chain on a Miniature Pinscher, nor would you put a thread on a Rottweiler.

Some breeds, such as all Setters and all Spaniels, are shown stacked with leads off. Most breeds, however, are shown with leads on. It is a matter of fashion. In the Junior ring, it is permissible to leave your show leads on the dog, but you should become adept at rolling them up in your hand so they are not dangling in the dog's face or your face, or wound around your legs. While you are baiting you will have the lead in your left hand and the bait in your right hand. Let out just enough lead to keep the head positioned where you want it and the rest rolled up in your hand—that is, unless you are showing a German Shepherd Dog. The custom in the Shepherd ring is to have folds of lead dangling. This is one of those customs which probably evolved when one successful handler did it, perhaps even inadvertently, and since the handler won with the dog, everyone else started to copy that technique. It might be interesting to see what would happen if you did not let your lead hang down between you and the dog, and you won. Chances are you could start another trend!

You will see all kinds of fancy manipulations with the leads in the conformation ring, but you should stick to the lead position that is easiest for you. Dogs react to leads differently, and you may have to experiment with someone watching you to tell you which lead makes the dog respond best. Some dogs hate the sound of a chain and will not gait, but if the lead is changed to nylon or cotton it makes all the difference in the world. Other dogs are not affected at all by the sound of the chain or the feel of certain materials around their necks.

Whether you free-bait or hard stack your dog, you must have control of the head, either with your hands or through the lead. If you allow the dog to lunge, drag, turn around or sniff you will have lost the ball game before you even begin to play. *Teaching the dog to stack is an important first step in control.*

If you have a breed that is customarily examined on a table, it is a good idea to first teach it to stack on the ground. You will have to do both in the ring. After your dog is standing well on terra firma, you can both "move up" to a grooming table and repeat the process there. Most dogs used to being groomed on a table do not mind being stacked there. In fact, it is usually easier for those dogs to be hard stacked than for others.

GAITING

Once you have mastered the intricacies of stacking, you can teach your dog to gait. It is a good idea to separate the two lessons so that the dog does not get confused about whether you want it to stand or go. In order to teach your dog to gait, you have to learn how to do it yourself. Try running in a straight line without weaving, tripping or looking down while holding your right arm perpendicular to the ground. Then do this same exercise holding a lead in your hand. Then practice running with one eye on your dog, one eye ahead of you and one eye on the judge! If you counted three, you're right, but that is how your attention must be divided in the ring. You have to know what your dog is doing, where you are going, so you don't run into tent poles or other people, and where the judge is so that you can return directly to the spot you left without weaving all over the ring.

Being young and presumably nimble will help in this exercise. Try going down and back, running in a triangle, doing an "L" and, finally, running in a circle the size of the average ring. If yours is a small breed in which sprinting is not required, practice at the proper speed for your dog.

Gaiting Patterns

Once you have mastered the formations it is time to attach your dog to a lead and gait slowly through each pattern. First, do the **down-and-back**, staying on your course and not allowing your dog to stray from your side. You might draw a chalk line, or lay a string so that you can tell if you look as though you were sober or needed a breath test. You will go away from the judge in a straight

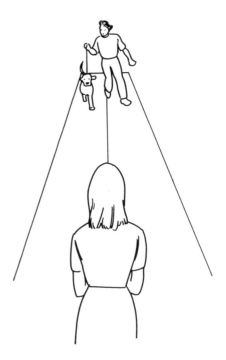

Gaiting Down and Back. The handler goes straight away from the judge and returns on the same line. *(Drawing by Pam Powers Zelenz)*

line to the end of the ring, then turn to the left and return in the same line as you went out. The dog remains on your left side as you return to where the judge would be standing.

Some people change hands in the corner so that the dog comes back on the right side, but that is awkward and requires unnecessary movement. As you return, look up to estimate how far you are from the judge and slow down so that you come to a stop about three feet from where the judge is standing. You do not want to race to a dead stop so that you and the dog are skidding into the judge and you both look as if you were running a marathon. Often down-and-backs are done on the diagonal across the ring because it gives you more room, but you must be alert to the judge's instructions and go where he or she tells you to go.

The **triangle** is perhaps the most popular gaiting pattern and one that is fairly easy to accomplish. However, you have to be alert to the corners. You will start straight away from the judge to the nearest corner, turn the dog on your left side and cross to the far

92

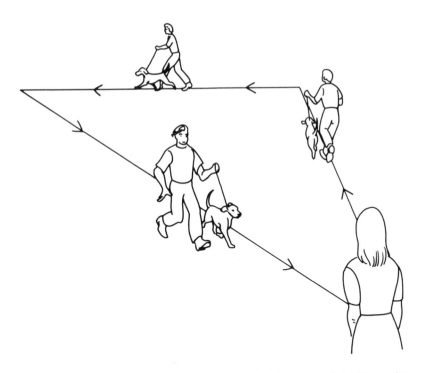

Gaiting in a Triangle. The handler moves away from the judge in a straight line to the end of the ring, turns smartly at the corner, crosses the far side of the ring and returns to the judge, keeping the dog always on the left side.

(Drawing by Pam Powers Zelenz)

side of the ring. Then come back to the judge on the diagonal, as you did for the down-and-back.

Occasionally, the judge will ask for the **"L"** pattern. Often this is done after the initial judging is completed, as it separates the "men from the boys," or "girls from the women." It becomes tricky, because it involves changing hands at the far end of the ring so that you come back with the dog on your right side, always keeping the dog between you and the judge. You will proceed straight to the end of the ring, turn and go across the ring, change hands in the corner, moving the dog in toward you and to your right side. Then proceed back across the far end of the ring. When you get to the corner you may either keep the dog on your right, or you may change hands again, turning the dog in toward you so it is on your left, and proceed to the judge.

You will find that in the breed ring most handlers do not change

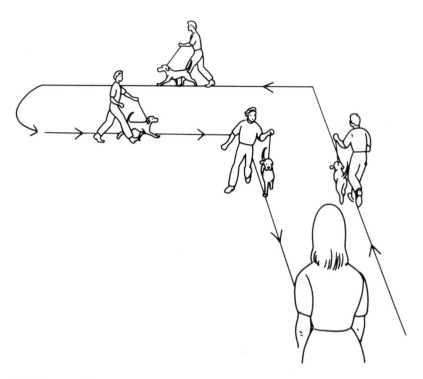

The "L" pattern is most cumbersome. The handler goes away from the judge in a straight line, crosses the far side of the ring. At the far corner he/she may switch hands while turning the dog to gait back across the ring. Many handlers, however, do not switch hands because in the conformation ring this is rarely done.

(Drawing by Pam Powers Zelenz)

hands to do the "L" but in Junior Showmanship it will be expected in order to emphasize the Cardinal Rule: **ALWAYS KEEP THE DOG BETWEEN YOU AND THE JUDGE.** The fact that it is an awkward pattern and rarely used does not mean you should ignore it. Someday it might mean the difference between winning and losing.

You will also need to practice gaiting in a **circle**. That may seem easy, but it is not. This is because you must keep a steady pace over a considerable distance, with the dog on your left and without cutting corners. Most handlers lose control of their dogs on the corners by letting them swing too wide into the circle. If anything, bring your dog closer to you as you approach the corners by folding in a little bit of the lead. As you head across the ring let out the lead so that your dog shows a smooth and fluid side gait going around.

94

This young lady steps out with her Brittany at the proper speed.

Practice your gaiting patterns with your dog one at a time. Do not mix them up in the same lesson or you will thoroughly confuse your dog, and yourself. Practice gaiting about ten minutes a day and when you feel comfortable with the patterns, invite a parent or friend to watch you to see how your dog looks from the judge's point of view.

THE TOTAL PICTURE

Once you have mastered both the stack and the gait you can put them together by practicing an entire routine just as you would in the ring. Gait in a circle, stack your dog, gait individually with your dog and, finally, gait again in a circle.

If there are Junior classes being held in your area by a local club it is a good idea to participate if your dog is old enough. You do not want to drag your puppy through weeks of classes while it is teething or it will end up fighting you, fighting the lead and hating every moment. There is time enough for classes when the puppy is older. You are better off working for short stretches at home and keeping it fun for you and the dog.

You could take your puppy to some Matches for practice and ring experience. These are better than classes because you will be in the ring for a short period of time and you can gain some knowledge without undue stress on the puppy. At the same time, they closely simulate the real thing.

Above all, keep it fun! This is a *sport* for you and your dog. If you are uptight and anxious your dog will feel it right away and reflect your anxieties. It will fidget and become uncooperative because it senses something is wrong. Stay calm and collected. Be reassuring to your dog. The best way to achieve that state of nirvana is to know the basic routines so that you do not have to think about every move every minute. Your stacking and gaiting routines should be automatic so that you can concentrate on the finer points of showing off your dog. You should be able to roll up your lead and let it out in your sleep. You should be able to remove the lead and put it back on your dog in an instant without fiddling. If you use bait, practice taking it out and putting it away in a pocket unobtru-

Gaiting in a circle gives a moving picture of each team.

sively and quickly. If you can master all these details, you'll have nothing to worry about when you get into the ring. The judge will notice what a smooth performer you are.

All breeds have some little characteristic in showing that will alert the judge to your degree of familiarity with it. As an example, a Lhasa Apso is shown with the tail curled over the back. In setting up the dog on the table you must be able to arrange the tail so that it is shown according to the custom for the breed. If you ignore the tail and it droops, not only will the dog look bad, but you will have demonstrated to the judge that your knowledge of how to show a Lhasa is incomplete.

Dogs with upright ears, such as the Akita or Shiba Inu, must have their ears forward and alert. You should learn where to place your hands behind the dog's ears with a slight pressure to push the ears forward and up. If you do this, you will demonstrate your knowledge of how those breeds should be shown to their best advantage.

Every dog is an individual, even those within a breed. To be a really good handler you must know your dog intimately and you must learn by observation how successful handlers in your breed show their dogs.

This Junior is hard-stacking his Miniature Schnauzer on the table for the judge's examination.

8

Attending Your First Show

THERE ARE BASICALLY two kinds of dog shows: Match and point. Match shows are run just like point shows but with the big difference that no championship points are awarded. Match shows are like practice events for young puppies or for inexperienced older dogs. They are also good training grounds for novice handlers. Classes are usually small and the atmosphere is much more relaxed. No one cares if a dog or a handler goofs up at a Match show, so it is a good place to begin to show your puppy.

Point shows come in all sizes from small five-hundred-dog shows to enormous four-thousand-dog shows. Points are awarded to dogs in each breed depending upon the number being shown that day. (See the Glossary for an explanation of the AKC point system.)

Before you begin to show your dog you should visit a show in your area. It is a good idea to go to a point show *to observe*, rather than a Match because the point show is where you will eventually compete. Depending upon the area of the country and the season, shows will be held either indoors or outdoors. You can call the American Kennel Club for a list of show-giving clubs in your region.

Call the Secretary of the club to find out when the show will be held. The week before the show, call to find out when Juniors will be exhibiting so you will be sure to be there at the right time. *Do not take your dog. Go just to observe.* Spend some time at ringside watching how people show their dogs. Watch your breed being judged and take note of how the handlers present their dogs. Watch how they stack them, either on the ground or on a table, and how they gait. You will find that different judges ask for different gaiting patterns, and you will have to learn them all.

LOOK, ASK, LISTEN, LEARN

Go under the grooming tent, or into the grooming section, and watch your breed being prepared. Most handlers will be happy to answer any questions you may have, so long as they are not about to dash off to show a dog.

Do not leave for the mall the minute your breed has been judged or Juniors are over. Stay and watch other breeds. You will learn a lot about the different types and varieties, and you may pick up some handling tips which could help you later on.

You should also observe at least one or two Groups, particularly your own. Eventually you may want to take your puppy, or another, into breed and, hopefully, Group competition. You'll need to know how to show your dog in the Group. Such subtle things as where it will stand in line, how the judges examine the dogs in the Group, how they are gaited, selected and finally placed are all important to know ahead of time. You will want to store that information away as you begin your Junior show career.

You will need to use your powers of observation to learn how best to show your dog.

- What kind of leads should you buy?
- What kind of brushes, combs and other accoutrements do you need?
- Is yours a breed that is hard stacked or free-baited or both?
- What kind of bait do other handlers use?
- Before you even begin to show your dog you will need to know the most basic thing: Where do you put your hands?
- Do you hold the head and the tail, just the head or just the tail?

This Junior is intently watching the judging from outside the ring.

- Do you stand in front of the dog or to the side?
- Do you stand up or kneel down?
- How do you hold the lead? Is it rolled up in your hand or extended out to the end?

Each breed has its fashions and quirks and every dog responds a little differently to the signals given both verbally and through body language by the handler. You will need to experiment with your dog to see what works best, but before you can do that you have to observe others so that you know what to try.

Chances are you will not be going to shows alone. You will be with your parent or a friend who knows something about the rules, the procedures and how the show is run. They can help you understand some of the unfathomable things that seem to go on as you see people rushing about from ring to ring, or standing around outside a ring waiting for what seems to be a longer time than the line for a rock concert ticket.

After you have visited a Match or two, you can bring your puppy. If you want to enter a show, try to select one where competition is small, so that you are not overwhelmed by being in a class with thirty other Juniors. Match shows generally do not need to be preentered and are usually small and informal. They are also considerably less expensive to enter than point shows, a definite consideration while you are learning the bare bones of showmanship.

You must preenter point shows through a Show Secretary or Superintendent. Shows are listed in the events calendar of Purebred Dogs *American Kennel Gazette*. (See "Useful Addresses" in the appendix for the address.) Once you have entered a show or two you will most likely be added to the show's mailing list for the following year.

THE DOG COMES FIRST

The most important thing to remember in showing your dog is that **the comfort and safety of your dog comes first**. No matter how much you are looking forward to the day, if your dog is not feeling well, don't show it. If it is very hot, be particularly careful about your dog's ability to adjust to the heat. It will be up to you to notice if the dog appears to be panting heavily, unable to gait or stand normally, and it is your responsibility to remove the dog from the ring or from the grooming tent and seek veterinary attention right away. Even though adults may be present, it is your dog and *you* must take care of it.

The same goes for some of the delicate breeds if it is very cold or wet. If the dog is uncomfortable, shivering and miserable there is no point in showing anyway. You just have to chalk it up as an experience and return another day.

No matter what, **THE DOG COMES FIRST!**

WHAT TO BRING

You might as well get used to the idea that you have to carry a lot of stuff when you go to a show. In addition to the dog, you

An awning for shade, grooming tables and a water jug are some of the amenities of dog showing.

should have some kind of carry **crate** and a **grooming table**. The reason a crate is a good idea is that you can put the dog into it, either in your car, if it is cool enough and safe, or inside at the show or outside under the tent, and the dog will rest comfortably until it is time to prepare it for the ring. Dogs who are dragged around the show grounds for hours before being shown become tired and bored. By the time they are ready to go into the ring they are worn out, lagging and definitely not looking good.

A grooming table will allow you to brush out your dog easily and will give you a place to keep the rest of your stuff. This will consist of a container, either a **tack box** or some other box (a fishing tackle box makes an excellent tack box), into which you will put all your necessary items:

- brushes
- combs
- an extra lead
- some rubber bands in case none are available to fasten your armband
- a tube of ointment in case of bee stings
- a little money for a soda and a snack

There are lots of other things that people put into their tack boxes, but you can add to these basics yourself.

Crates stacked in a van make it easy to travel and comfortable for the dogs.

A hair dryer is being used on this Irish Setter for a last minute touch-up.

Very Important: You will also need to bring water for the dog and a bowl and some bait—whatever treat your dog likes best.

Make a list of things to bring before you go. Try to consider everything you might need for yourself and your dog so that you don't end up at every show mooching from your fellow exhibitors. Most kids are pretty generous, but those who are always unprepared can become tiresome after a while.

AT THE SHOW

Plan to arrive at the show in plenty of time before judging to situate yourself and your dog comfortably. At a Match, you may not know ahead of time when Juniors will be judged, although some information flyers do give a time schedule. Your point show judging schedule will tell you when your classes are scheduled and in what ring they will be judged. Try to set up close to the ring in which you will be judged so that you can take your dog off the grooming table to the ring without traversing the entire show site.

Once you are settled, either go to purchase a catalog (point shows publish catalogs listing all exhibitors and dogs being shown that day) or borrow one from a friend. Check to see that you and your dog are correctly listed in the catalog in the proper class. Sometimes mistakes are made by the Superintendent or Show Secretary, and you may find that you have been entered in the wrong class. If this happens you should immediately inform either of these persons so that the judge's book is marked right and the catalog listing corrected. Otherwise, if you compete in the wrong class in Juniors and win, you might be disqualified from that win.

As the time draws closer for your class to be judged, go ahead of time to the ring to get your armband. At a Match, you receive your armband when you register and pay your fee. At a point show, you receive your number in the mail; your armband will be waiting for you in custody of the ring steward in the ring in which you will be judged. A lot of exhibitors never bother to look up their entry before they go to the steward's table. This means they or the steward have to look up the number in the catalog, holding up the other exhibitors who are waiting for their numbers. It is courteous to know your number before you get there.

After you have gotten your armband and affixed it to your left arm, try to determine how long the wait will be until your class is called. Since you will probably be in Novice, your class may be the first one called, but there will usually be conformation classes being held in your ring ahead of Juniors.

You can ask the ring steward or consult your judging program to see how many classes are ahead of you. If there is a lot of time, try to find the judge who is scheduled for Juniors and watch that person conduct another ring. Although judges of Juniors sometimes vary their patterns, regulations state that Juniors should be judged just as any other class.

You can anticipate how Juniors will be judged by observing your judge handle a conformation class. If you are not the first class of Juniors, by all means watch the preceding classes to learn what pattern the judge is asking for. Remember, in Junior Showmanship particularly, following the judge's instructions is very important! You may be forgiven other things, but if you ignore what the judge tells you to do, you will have lost, for sure.

You will learn to estimate how much time you need to exercise and brush out your dog before you show it, but allow enough time to walk the dog, make sure it relieves itself in a proper place, give it some water and then put it on the grooming table.

Your dog will learn to anticipate that being brushed and fussed over at a show means "show time." Whether that is a pleasurable experience or a drag will be up to you. Your attitude, the way you brush and comb your dog and encourage it with your tone of voice will tell the dog that this is going to be a lot of fun. Later in this book we will give you some hints about how to have a happy dog in the show ring, but your preparations ahead of time will make a big difference in how the dog looks forward to what will happen next.

Finally, the time arrives for you to go up to the ring with your dog. Put the show lead on while the dog is on the table, put your bait in the bait pocket of your skirt or pants, give your own hair a final brush and straighten your clothes before you set out.

You will enter the ring in the order in which the steward instructs you. Some judges want the dogs in catalog order, so you will stand according to your armband number. Others don't care in what order you enter the ring. If it is a large class, the judge may

This young lady has complete control of her dog. She is keeping the dog occupied with a treat while she waits for her class to be called.

have everyone enter in catalog order and then he or she may separate the class into sections. It may be divided into groups of eight or ten, or it may be divided by the size of the dogs. In Juniors, judges may decide it is easier if dogs of similar size are gaited together. In that way, a Junior with a large Poodle is not stuck behind one with a Chihuahua. No matter what the judge decides, *follow instructions*.

If the class is divided, notice who is in front of you and who is behind you, so while you wait you will remember where you belong in the line when you are called into the ring for your turn.

While you are waiting your turn, watch the judge and watch the competition. See what others are doing and try to evaluate whether they are doing a good job, or what you would do differently. At the same time, be attentive to your dog and keep the dog under control at all times. Do not allow your dog to sniff at the other dogs in the ring or on the sidelines. Do not allow a dog to become overly excited or fidgety while standing. Talk quietly or use your hands to gently stroke and calm your dog.

Do not use your time in the ring to gab with your competitors. Stay focused on your dog and on the judge. You will find that the more you concentrate the better and smoother your performance will be and the better your dog will behave.

Above all, remember: You and your dog are a team from the time you leave the grooming area until you leave the ring, either a winner or a loser.

9

Show Time!

YOU HAVE DONE your homework, practiced at home with your dog, and now it is time to take the plunge and enter a show. Find out from a friend, mentor, breeder or parent when and where shows will be held in your area. Do this well ahead of the time you plan to be ready with your dog. Otherwise you will miss the closing date for entries, which can be three to six weeks ahead of the event. If possible, enter a small show where there are likely to be fewer Juniors in competition. By doing this you will get the experience but will not have the added stress of waiting for a long time to be judged. Your dog will remain fresh and interested in everything going on around you both.

After the basic lessons you learned at home, you must have ring experience to become proficient and have confidence in yourself and in your dog. Do not expect great things to happen the first time you step into a ring, no matter how prepared you think you are. Just the fact of being at a real show with other competitors more experienced than you can be somewhat intimidating. Butterflies in your stomach can cause you to make mistakes which you have never even thought of at home. Don't despair! Everyone goes through it, and not only in Junior Showmanship.

IN THE RING

When your class is called to the ring, listen for instructions from the steward. If you are requested to go in catalog order, then you have no choice but to obey. If you have a choice, however, try to position yourself advantageously. For example, if you have a small dog, go to the back of the line, so that you will not be trampled by a large dog running up on yours. Also, if you have a small dog, do not place it between two behemoths or it will certainly get lost to the judge's view, not to mention becoming fearful at the large creatures bearing down on it from either end.

If you have a large or medium-sized dog, try not to be first in line. Let someone who knows the way lead off. You can follow and learn the routine from the person ahead of you.

This Junior is focused on his Miniature Pinscher and vice versa.

After all exhibitors are checked in, the judge will evaluate the class and decide how it will be divided. As previously mentioned, if there are only a few entries, chances are you will all remain in the ring and the judge may ask the large dogs to go ahead of the small ones. If you are part of a large class, the judge may ask half the class to wait outside the ring while the first half is judged and some excused before the second half is brought in. Listen to the judge's instructions, watch the exhibitors ahead of you, so that when it is your turn you do not have to ask the judge where to stand, where to gait and what pattern is being used. Usually the judge will repeat instructions with every child, but he or she may decide not to do that, testing whether you have been paying attention to what is going on in the ring.

If you are in the ring waiting your turn, keep focused on your dog. The dog does not have to remain hard stacked or free-baited the whole time, especially in a large class, but you must be working at control and making your dog look alert, attentive and interested in

While waiting, he keeps his dog interested and alert by a little playing.

This young lady sets up her Dalmatian . . .

makes a picture for the judge and . . .

112

. . . shows the bite as the judge approaches the dog from the front.

The judge then examines the dog's neck and shoulder from the side.

you. When the person ahead of you goes to set up his/her dog, you should be ready to stack your dog, making sure Chipper looks his best.

The first thing you will do is to **stand the dog** for the judge to examine it. If it is a table breed, as soon as the person ahead of you starts a gaiting pattern, put your dog on the table and stack it to be completely ready for the judge. If it is a breed that is examined on the ground, go to the place that the person ahead of you has just left and stack your dog.

Examination

The judge will begin evaluating your dog by looking at it from the side from a short distance away. Then he or she will move to the front to examine the head, teeth, neck and shoulders. You may let go of the head if the judge has taken control of it. If not, always hold the head or, if a free-baited breed, keep the lead tight around the neck so that the dog does not swing around, dive for the ground or twist into a "U" shape. Once the judge has released the head, you must be right there to hang on to it.

The judge's hands will run down the dog's body to the hindquarters. You may move to the head of the dog, or you may stand at its side, holding the head until the examination is complete. Do not drop the lead *or* drop your hands and let your dog stand there on its own. If the dog does not decide to exit the ring at that moment, it certainly will not look too good. You will appear inattentive and confused. The judge may at that point go around to the other side of the dog. If that happens, as soon as the judge passes over the midpoint of the dog, you must go around to the other side, remembering the Cardinal Rule: **ALWAYS KEEP THE DOG BETWEEN YOU AND THE JUDGE!**

Gaiting

Once the individual examination is complete the judge will indicate where you should gait the dog. **Follow instructions!** Although the guidelines state that every dog must be examined in the same way, it is possible that the judge may like to fool people by changing the gaiting pattern.

Gather your lead in your left hand, so that the extra lengths

Listening to the judge's instructions is essential. This young lady and her Collie are attentive.

are not dangling (unless you are showing a German Shepherd) and set out at a smart pace. Juniors are expected to do a courtesy turn in front of the judge, although this maneuver is no longer done in the breed ring. Hopefully, it will be eliminated from Junior Showmanship some day as well.

The courtesy turn is done by stepping out in front of the judge, turning in a circle so that the dog remains on your left side and then setting off down the ring. The only really good reason for ever doing a courtesy turn is to settle down an unruly dog, but since it is expected, you should prepare to do it.

When you return to the judge from your individual gaiting pattern, he or she will instruct you as to what to do next. You may be told to gait to the end of the line, in which case you will take your dog in a modified circle (no need to run the entire ring) to the end. The judge may place every member of the class, and tell you to stand in a certain spot (behind the Dalmatian and in front of the Bichon, for example). In that event, just walk to the designated

After she has finished her individual gaiting pattern she waits for the rest of the class to be judged.

116

place at a brisk pace with your dog held firmly in check. When you get there, if the people in front and in back have not moved to make room for you, politely explain that the judge has placed you here. The whole line will then adjust their positions as the judge shuffles the deck.

Teamwork

While you are going through your routine, the judge will be evaluating how you relate to your dog. Remember that you should have learned the basics of stacking and gaiting, so that those moves become almost automatic. How you and your dog interact, however, is never automatic. Your dog will be influenced by everything around it and everything inside it, and you must be able to understand and work with the mood of the animal at that moment. Maybe the dog will be reacting to your mood or your nervousness. You must show a great deal of patience and calmness in the ring with your dog.

Not only are jerky motions, displays of anger or impatience or heavy-handedness penalized by the judge, but these are destructive elements in the relationship between you and your dog.

Patience is one of the hardest things Juniors have to learn. Without this quality you will never be a top Junior Handler. Patience with your dog, with yourself when you make the inevitable mistakes, and with the seemingly endless waiting for things to happen are all part of the sport. You have to learn to go with the flow in order to succeed.

While you are doing all this patient waiting, use the time to observe how others are showing their dogs. You can learn a great deal just by watching, not only what Juniors are doing right, but what they are doing wrong. Do not use your time, either in the ring (especially in the ring) or outside it, to gab with your friends, snack, drink sodas that can spill on your dog's coat (or some other dog) or daydream. Be attentive to how your dog looks and what he or she is doing. You do not want your dog bothering other dogs, or being annoyed by others. It is up to you to control the space that you and your dog occupy.

DRESS FOR THE OCCASION

The guidelines for Juniors state that clothes should be neat, clean and appropriate. Add conservative to that. You are not supposed to be making a fashion statement when you walk into the show ring. *Your dog must be the center of attention*, and the less obvious you are, the more you will impress the judge. Girls should be attired in a simple skirt or dress, with pockets. If you wear a sweater or jacket, keep it buttoned, so it will not swing in your dog's face. Skirts should be of moderate length, no minis, please, and should not be voluminous or you may hide your dog as you run. When you are buying your skirt, bend over and take a look in the rearview mirror. Don't forget, your back will be to the ringside a lot of the time! If you are planning to wear a low-cut blouse, bend over in the front. Appropriate attire, remember, is the key. Leave

Attire should be neat and comfortable. This girl is wearing a jumper which allows free movement, but does not interfere with the dog. Her hair is done up in a pony tail. The young man is correctly dressed in a suit and tie.

the bangle jewelry at home and tie up long hair into a bun or ponytail. It should not be swishing in your face, or that of your dog. The judge does not want to see your hair, as lovely as it is, and you should not spend a minute fussing with it in the ring.

Boys should wear a jacket and pants, no jeans. If it is very hot, and the judge is no longer wearing a jacket, it is permissible to show without one. However, always come prepared to wear one. Older boys should wear ties which are held in place by tie tacks or holders. They should not be dangling over your dog.

Shoes should not be the latest flimsy sandals or slippery moccasins. They should be serviceable, easy to run in and comfortable. Sneakers, boat shoes or other moderately styled athletic shoes are perfect. Huge, clunky sneakers with the laces dragging on the ground are definitely out of place.

Loud patterns on jackets or skirts detract from your dog. The only contrast you should consider is a solid color which allows the dog to show up against you. If you have a black dog you'll want to wear a light-colored skirt or pants. Dark clothes will make your dog invisible next to you. Although most judges will not penalize a Junior for some inappropriate article of clothing, the entire picture that you present makes an impression on the judge. At the large and prestigious shows, dress certainly plays a part in the whole presentation.

FINESSE—NOT FUSS

The guidelines stress that Juniors who display a smooth way of handling their dogs with economy of motion and little wasted effort should be rewarded. Easy to say, hard to accomplish!

You can achieve that goal if you remember that every motion must have a reason. Do not fuss with any part of the dog without knowing beforehand why you are doing it. Did you need to move that foot? Adjust that lead? Turn the dog around? Jerk the head up? You will find that many of the moves you make are really unnecessary and only serve to call attention to yourself. You want to develop the habit of *quiet hands*.

Watch professional handlers in the conformation rings. You will see that they rarely touch their dogs. In fact, some of them look as though they are not doing anything but standing there. However, they know exactly what their dogs are doing and can quickly and smoothly change a position if they need to.

Many Juniors attempt to copy the moves which professionals in their breeds make. As mentioned, that is usually a mistake unless you know exactly why a handler is doing a certain thing. You are better off developing your own style to suit your needs than becoming a carbon copy of someone else, for no good reason. in fact, you can open yourself up to ridicule. "Have you seen Joe, he's trying to look just like Mr. Professional Cool!" Judges notice those things, too, and are usually not impressed.

Quiet hands, economy of motion, smoothness. These are all comforting terms, relaxing terms, compared to the frantic antics which many inexperienced exhibitors demonstrate in the ring. This is the goal you should strive for in Junior Showmanship, and it will take you far in breed competition later on.

10

Sportsmanship and Other Good Things

ONE OF THE STATEMENTS of purpose in the Guidelines for Juniors is "to experience winning and losing among those who are similar in age." Winning with humility and losing with grace are the definition of good sportsmanship. It is difficult to be modest when you have won a huge class. It is even harder to grit your teeth, smile and congratulate the winner after you have lost. It is especially tough to be gracious if you know you have done a good job and you feel you should have won.

You have to remember that judging is a subjective thing. It is not like math, where there is only one right answer. What you see and what the judge sees may vary, but it is the judge's opinion that counts in the show ring. No one goes into competition of any sort to lose, but it happens to everyone from the rank novice to the most seasoned professional in every sport.

Second-guessing is useless, but honestly evaluating your performance, thinking about what you might have done better, is the only way you will improve the next time. Sometimes Junior Showmanship judges will gather the class after it is over and explain why

Judging is a subjective thing. Here the judge walks down the line in a class in order to get a final impression.

they placed their winners as they did. They will usually tell the class what the winners did that was right, rather than dwell on what the losers did that was wrong. You will then have to figure out what you did not do compared to the winner's performance. If your parent or trusted friend is at ringside you might ask them for an evaluation. If you wish to go further you may ask the judge after all Junior Showmanship classes are through what you can do to improve. Do not ask what you did wrong. Ask what you can do better. Judges sometimes do not like to answer these personal questions, because they do not want to get into a discussion about you. Sometimes they just don't remember every child in a large class.

You will learn more about yourself by observing others and comparing their performance to yours than you will by asking questions of the judge.

If you have won, accept the congratulations of your competitors gracefully. Nobody likes a braggart, so save your gloating until you are in the car on the way home, with the windows rolled up. The same goes if you lose. Never criticize the competition while you are anywhere near the show grounds. You never know who is listening, but you can be sure it is the winner's best friend!

When you win first place accept your ribbon and trophy from the judge with a polite thank-you. If you win second, third or fourth you will do the same, with an even broader smile. You will not throw your ribbon on the ground or in the trash can, you will not stomp out of the ring and, above all, **you will never, ever blame your dog by word or deed when you lose**. Not only does that demonstrate extremely poor sportsmanship, but someone might file a complaint against you and you could be suspended from showing your dog at any shows for months.

THE PARENTS' ROLE

Sportsmanship extends to your family, too. Your parents have encouraged you to participate in Junior Showmanship. Most likely they have helped you train your dog, and they are the ones who do the driving, pay the entry fees and rejoice when you win. They are also expected to be good sports when you lose. Nothing is more embarrassing to a Junior, nor annoying to a judge, than to be berated by an angry parent when the child does not win.

She awards first place to a young lady with a Boxer.

124

All of the same elements of winning and losing which you are expected to respect also apply to your parents. They are expected to congratulate the winner and the winner's parents, and they should realize that losing a class is not the end of the world. There is always another show. Parents can help their Juniors best by offering constructive suggestions away from the ring. All of you can work at home to improve performance. Do not stand at ringside offering advice or shouting suggestions across the ring.

If parents are incapable of standing quietly, they would be doing a service to their offspring by disappearing, going to watch a breed at the other end of the show grounds, finding a friend with a motor home and watching the ball game until the class is over. One father, who was a professional handler, made it a rule never to stand at ringside to watch his daughter. Once in a while he could be seen several rings away, glancing over to see what was happening, but all comments were made away from the show.

Parents should never enter the ring to confront the judge. Not only is it an embarrassment to the child, but it is liable to bring a formal complaint from the judge, resulting in a fine or suspension by AKC. Parents should set an example of good sportsmanship for their children, fostering good habits which will carry over into the conformation ring.

BEYOND YOUR CONTROL?

It is important to repeat: **Never, ever** take your disappointment out on your dog, either in the ring or out. It is true that sometimes dogs act like delinquents, refusing to do the simplest thing correctly. Punishment after the fact will accomplish nothing, because the dog will not understand why you are angry. Punishment, or any display of temper in the ring, will surely get you disqualified. If your dog is acting like a jerk, sometimes there is nothing you can do except grit your teeth and bear it until the class is over. It is also possible that a little extra practice beforehand would have prevented the problem.

On the other hand, judges are very impressed with Juniors who are able to take a difficult dog and handle it with aplomb. Even though you may not be able to turn in the best performance of your

This girl has to really step out with her Saluki.   (Photo by Michael Baker)

life, if you are able to get the dog under control and working with you as a team, the judge will certainly notice. The judge will also notice if you become flustered, angry or impatient with your dog.

After the ordeal is over, try to analyze why your dog misbehaved. Was there a bitch in season in the next ring? Was the weather a factor? Was the dog not feeling well? Was someone tossing bait near you? Did you remember to exercise your dog beforehand so that it would not want to relieve itself in the ring? Were you using a different show lead? Were you trying out some new fancy footwork that the dog had never seen before? Were you nervous or apprehensive about the class? All of these things and many more affect your dog's performance in the ring.

Yelling at a dog after the fact accomplishes nothing. It will, however, give you a bad reputation among your competitors.

One of the most difficult things for Juniors to learn is how to read their dog. Dogs have moods, just like people. Some more than others, but dogs are affected by external things which will cause

126

them to react differently under situations with which they should be very familiar.

If you see that your dog is not behaving well, and you have done your homework, so that the dog knows the routine and what you expect, then you have to find out the reason for the bad behavior. We have described some factors which may cause some dogs to act up in the ring, but you can imagine that there are many other reasons as well.

Once you have figured out what the problem might be, it will be too late to do anything about it on that day. This does not mean that you should go home and forget about it and hope it does not happen again. In addition to knowing what the problem is, you must work with your dog to find a solution.

PROOF TRAINING—FINDING SOLUTIONS

Suppose your dog freaked out because it was windy and the tents were flapping. It would be your instinct to be reassuring and say, "Good dog, that's okay." What you are then actually saying is that it's fine to freak out at the sound of the tents. What you really want to do is get your dog used to the tents flapping, so you should quietly walk around outside the tents, not saying much, just going along as if nothing was wrong. When calmed down, the dog should then get lots of extra praise for not being afraid.

With any situation you have to figure out what the problem is and the most effective way of correcting it. Every dog responds differently to stimuli. You have to experiment with a lot of techniques to discover what works for your dog.

Take bait, for example. When you are working at home, you might find that your dog is up on its toes and practically lunging for the treat in your hand. So you figure that is what will make it a star in the show ring. When you get into the ring, however, the dog totally ignores you and refuses to even sniff at the bait. There is so much more going on that food is the last thing the dog will focus on. You have to have alternate plans ready to put into action if that happens.

If the dog is fascinated by a lady's hat at ringside, get closer so your dog can have a look at it. There's nothing wrong with using

This exhibitor is concentrating completely on her Boxer, so she will know how the dog will react to various distractions.

whatever trick is available as long as the dog looks good and doesn't bother anyone else. Many exhibitors use squeaky toys to attract their dog's attention. This is fine, as long as it does not disturb the dogs around you. If you are distracting the other dogs, however, you are being discourteous to your fellow exhibitors. You should recognize this before someone asks you to please refrain from squeaking your toy. On the other hand, you might be able to use someone else's annoying sounds to your own advantage. If your dog comes alive at the sound, let the dog stand on its own. Just make sure that the stance and appearance is correct and that you look as though you know exactly what you are doing.

If you have a problem that you cannot solve, don't be afraid to ask someone knowledgeable in your breed for help. Most exhibitors are happy to help Juniors improve their skills, as long as they have a genuine interest in the sport and in their dogs.

SENDING A MESSAGE DOWN THE LEAD

Your dog will reflect your mood. If you are grumpy, sad or not feeling well, chances are that your friend will not be having much fun, either. It is up to you to set the tone for the day from the time you load up the car until the time you leave the show ring after the class is over.

To show successfully you must believe in your dog. You must feel that your dog is important and that you are proud to own and to exhibit this dog for all to see. You must display your dog as a prized possession, which, in fact, it is. Your dog will work for you if you give the attention and devotion it deserves and if the dog feels you demonstrate affection. Remember that a win or a loss does not change the dog. These things mean nothing to it. The dog that you bring into the ring is the same dog you will leave with. It is no better or worse for having won or lost. Dog shows are for people, not for dogs. Dogs do not care about a ribbon. They want only to please you.

If you look at Junior Showmanship as an opportunity to have fun with your dog, to compete in a friendly manner with those of your own age, then you will understand the meaning of good sportsmanship.

Some breeds are more difficult to prepare and handle than others. Here an exhibitor sets up an Afghan Hound. On size alone, this dog takes more hours to prepare than the Papillon at the end of the line. *(Photo by Michael Baker)*

11

Competitions and Conflicts

_____

THERE ARE MANY opportunities for Juniors to show their dogs in competition with their peers. There are Match Shows every week in most areas of the United States where Junior Showmanship classes are held for children aged eight to eighteen. These are given by all-breed kennel clubs and you can find out about them by getting a list of kennel clubs from the American Kennel Club.

These clubs also hold point shows, at least one, and some clubs hold two during the course of a year. Classes are held for Junior Showmanship at nearly all of them.

Specialty clubs also hold classes for Juniors at their shows. These are single-breed clubs devoted to the protection and betterment of one breed. If there is a local Specialty club for your breed in your area, it would be a good idea for you and your parents to join. You will learn a great deal about your breed and how to care for and handle it properly.

NATIONAL COMPETITION

There are two major national competitions for Juniors in the United States. The oldest is offered by the Westminster Kennel Club. Westminster was one of the first clubs to provide children's handling classes, and a win at this most prestigious show or to even qualify for it is important for Juniors.

In order to qualify to compete at Westminster, which is held at Madison Square Garden in New York City each February, a junior must win First Place awards in Open Junior Showmanship classes at eight shows during the course of one year. Elimination competition is held on the two evenings of Westminster (always a Monday and a Tuesday), and the finals, consisting of competition among all the previous class winners, is held on Tuesday evening. You can write to the Westminster Kennel Club for additional information about the competition. (See "Useful Addresses" in the Appendix for the address.)

The other major competition for Juniors is the World Series of Junior Showmanship. This is not only national in scope, but the winner of the competition in the United States goes on to compete with the winners of European Junior competitions through an all-expenses-paid trip to England.

The World Series is sponsored by Pedigree Dog Foods and produced by Newport Dog Show Superintendents. Juniors may qualify for the World Series by winning Best Junior at any one of many specifically designated shows held throughout the year in all parts of the country. The winners of those competitions meet at Beverly Hills Kennel Club in Pasadena, California, in June, and the winner of that goes to England to compete at one of the most prestigious shows in the world.

The competition at the World Series consists of three parts, an interview with a panel of judges selected to judge the competition, the class competition and then the finals. All competitors who have qualified to participate are given an expense-free trip to California for themselves, their dog and a chaperone, including a day of sight-seeing in southern California.

Winners who go to England to compete may not bring their own dogs because of quarantine regulations. For the initial competition they are provided with a dog of their own breed. They are then asked to switch to another breed to see how well they can adapt their handling techniques to other breeds.

Pedigree has made a major contribution to illustrating the importance of Junior Showmanship in the dog show world by sponsoring these competitions. They bring a focus to the Junior ring which had not been evident before this was started several years ago.

The level of competition at both Westminster and the World Series is consistently high. Juniors who win at any level in these shows have had to demonstrate a degree of proficiency which could match many professional handlers.

Judges who are selected to officiate at these shows must have demonstrated a knowledge of Junior Showmanship. Many were either professional handlers or Junior competitors themselves. Moreover, the majority are truly interested in Juniors and are versed in the rules and regulations which govern the sport.

They will look to reward those Juniors who handle themselves smoothly, calling attention to their dogs and not to themselves. They will try to pick as their winners handlers whom they think can compete effectively in the breed ring. Some use as their criteria: "Which Junior would I like to handle my dog?" Competition at this level is not for the faint of heart. Even entering a show to qualify for this level is like going into the ring for Best in Show every time. Juniors hoping to go into this kind of competition really must practice their skills with their dogs every day. This is not something that just happens by luck. It takes work and dedication, time and money. The rewards are significant, as in any sport, when you reach the top in terms of your own personal gain.

Personal Rewards

No phase of the dog show game brings significant monetary rewards. If you are looking for material gains, you will not find them here. You will find enormous satisfaction in participating in a sport which affords you the opportunity to compete with your peers, and also to create a real bond between you and your dog. You will make good friends from different parts of the country, and you will find that common interest in dogs will bring you together long after you have graduated out of Junior Showmanship.

Classes at Westminster are large and full of excellent competitors.

CONFLICTS

Juniors often find themselves with real conflicts, especially as they enter high school. They find themselves pulled in several directions, with all the different activities in which they would like to participate. This is particularly true for those teens who engage in sports at school. Football, basketball and soccer are major attractions for many youngsters, and the choice must be made between those activities and dog shows. It is almost impossible to belong to a team and go to shows at the same time. Homework, practice and games take too much time for children to do it all. One usually has to make the choice between one and another. It is possible to select one sport, say soccer, in the fall and then go to shows in the winter, spring and summer. Or baseball in the spring, basketball in the winter and shows summer and fall. It depends, of course, on what the main attractions are at the time.

Some Juniors are musicians, some actors, some artists. Some belong to the debating team. Some ride in horse shows. Juniors tend to be active in many things, as they should be at that age. The choice of whether to stick to dog shows or to participate in other things must belong to them. Parents should not force a child to participate in Junior Showmanship. The child must have a real interest in doing so. This is especially true as the child gets older and has choices to make.

There are some children who naturally gravitate to dog shows and who gladly put aside all other activities to be there. For most, however, dog shows become one thing that can occupy a weekend. When that becomes the case, it is important to allow the child to experience other things. Their training in the show ring will benefit them in many ways to participate in other sports. Their hand/eye coordination has been developed, they are usually in good physical shape, their sense of timing and balance has been nurtured and fine-tuned. They have learned good sportsmanship and how to relate well to others. Junior Showmanship will have played an important role in fitting them to be team players in almost any sport or activity they choose to try.

Parents who insist that children give up all other activities to go to shows usually find that the youngsters lose interest rapidly, not only in the shows themselves but in the dogs as well. Teens need to experiment with other things. Often they will return to the show ring later on, sometimes not until they are adults with dogs of their own, or at the point where they decide on a career. Young people may need that latitude and parents are wise to recognize this.

Parents who drag kids to shows just so they will have extra hands to fetch and carry are not going to create long-lasting interest in these children. In fact, the opposite may be true. Some children who have started off enthusiastically become bored and resentful when their own lives begin to come into focus. There needs to be a balance between the wishes of the parents and the desires of the child. This may seem like an obvious thing to say, but dog showing tends to become a consuming passion for some people in a family, but not always for all.

It may become a problem which needs to be discussed and compromises reached. There may be times when children absolutely cannot stay home if there is no one to look after the household. Children need to understand that there are circumstances such as this, if at other times they are free to pursue their independent activities. Children themselves must be able to make their decisions according to what is reasonable for the family and suitable for themselves in any particular year. Their interests will change and what was important last year becomes insignificant next year.

RESOLUTION

One of the lessons to be learned, however, is the need to stick to whatever activity they choose for a reasonable period of time. If they decide to show dogs in Junior Showmanship classes, they should stay with that decision at least long enough to become fairly adept so they have a chance of winning. Once they have become proficient in the sport it is up to them to decide whether they wish to continue with it or not. The same principle applies to whatever other endeavor they take up. If they choose to participate in a team sport, they should stay with that sport long enough and with sufficient dedication to learn it well enough to make an informed decision about whether to continue with it or to go on to something else.

With dog showing, the idea of continuity is particularly important because the Juniors are engaged not only by themselves but with their dogs. These animals are taught to expect a certain amount of attention, training, care and affection. They should not be discarded like an old football when the Junior moves on to something else. Even if the dog's show career is over when the Junior gives up the show lead, the dog's need for care and attention should not be abandoned. That is an ongoing responsibility they need to maintain.

There will come a time when Junior Showmanship is over. It might be at the eighteenth birthday when they are no longer eligible. It might be sooner, if other activities become more important. Whenever that time occurs, the needs of the dogs must be considered, too. They should not be left home in the kennel week after week while the children go off in one direction and the parents in another. These are show dogs and companions, too, and they deserve to be taken along for the ride, to the soccer game or to a show. They deserve to be put on the grooming table and fussed over from time to time, just as if they were still the stars they were before.

This is an important lessons for Juniors to learn. One does not discard one's friends, one's dependents or one's responsibilities, no matter what else is enticing at the time. If nothing else is learned from Junior Showmanship, this alone would make the sport worthwhile. This is the essential lesson which parents can teach their children, by word and by example.

A professional handler's set up at a show is like a home away from home.

12

Careers

IT MAY NOT SEEM POSSIBLE when you are twelve or thirteen, but there is life after Junior Showmanship. This reality comes about on your eighteenth birthday, when Juniors are no longer eligible to compete in these classes.

During the years in which Junior Showmanship has been part of your life, you will have learned a great deal about the dog show world and about dogs in general. The knowledge that you have gained will benefit you should you decide to pursue a career which is somehow related to animals.

There are many avenues Juniors can investigate before deciding on their life's work. Some require a great deal of additional education. Others require training or apprenticeship. It is safe to say that any career in any field may require a basic knowledge of business, accounting and computer skills. These should be at the core of any career decisions. They may not require a four-year college degree, but some post–high school education is almost mandatory for any meaningful job.

PROFESSIONAL HANDLER

The most obvious progression for career-minded Juniors is to continue in the dog show business as a professional handler. You will probably know by the time you "age-out" of Juniors whether this is appealing to you. You will have had experience in showing, grooming, handling. Hopefully, you will also have been involved in the daily routine of caring for your dog. Many Juniors follow in the footsteps of their professional-handler parents. These youngsters will have had ample hands-on experience to know whether life as a professional handler is appealing.

One must be physically and psychologically attuned to long hours on the road, a great deal of physical stress in hauling crates, setting up and taking down at shows, carrying dogs, kneeling, bending, lifting and generally putting one's body through a lot of abuse. Injuries to knees, ankles and backs are legion among dog handlers, whether amateur or professional.

Juniors who follow their parents have a step up on the career ladder, because they may be able to inherit some of the clients their parents have had over the years. It is not a certain thing, however, because new handlers always have to prove themselves capable of achieving on their own.

It is common practice among professionals for Juniors to apprentice with other handlers in order to get the experience and to have hands-on practice with different breeds of dogs. Professional handlers with a large number of dogs to show often have openings for assistant kennel help and assistance on the road. One former professional always insisted that his hired help spend months in the kennel before ever going on the road. This was in order for the employee to learn the daily routine of caring for show dogs before being permitted to travel and care for dogs at the shows.

More Than Meets the Eye

Most true professional handlers state that the work which goes on between shows when the dogs are at home in the kennel is far more important than what goes on at the shows. Dogs must be conditioned, bathed, exercised, fed a proper balanced diet, trained and constantly evaluated. All this is done before a show lead is ever placed around the dog's neck.

140

Assistants who are knowledgeable about all the facets of creating a top show dog are invaluable to any professional handler.

Professional handlers who manage the careers and breeding lives of their owners' dogs do more than just show them. They often play a role in the selection of the mates for these dogs. They whelp the puppies, care for and evaluate the litter, raise the young stock and train them for the show ring. A young person beginning a career as a professional can get invaluable experience from apprenticing to an established handler.

Apprenticing

The word "apprentice" has gone out of favor in the business/trade world. In the past, however, all professional handlers had to apprentice, and the best handlers, many of whom went on to become respected judges, apprenticed for several years to different handlers before striking out on their own.

It is not demeaning to be an apprentice. It no longer implies

At an indoor show, everything is brought in and arranged to work in a small space.

long hours at no pay. Assistants (which apprentices now call themselves) are usually paid a decent, though modest, wage and are usually supplied with rent-free living quarters. Some employers pay benefits, but this is rare. Most assistants remain with one professional for at least two years, unless there is personal animosity. This can happen with any job, of course, but since the assistant and the professional spend so much time together, six or seven days a week, it is almost imperative that they get along.

Assistants sometimes try to establish their own clients after two years, but it is more likely that they will work for two or three professionals before setting up their own business. By doing so they broaden their base of experience as well as meet prospective clients in many different breeds.

Becoming "Professional"

There are many people in the dog Fancy who call themselves professionals because they charge a fee for taking a dog into the ring. These are people who do not run a kennel, do not maintain dogs and do not condition or train them, and who often have other jobs during the week. These so-called professionals call themselves "agents" and they frequently undercut the fees charged by full-time professional handlers. They do not maintain an establishment devoted full time to dogs.

The technical training which we discussed earlier in this chapter is absolutely necessary for a professional handler in order to run a successful business. A working knowledge of accounting, bookkeeping and computer skills can make the difference between profit and loss. Professional handlers have a large overhead. They must pay for their buildings, house and kennel, vehicles, usually two including a van or motor home and a car, and all the insurance associated with these. They have a payroll to meet including the assistants and kennel help, which is maintained seven days a week. Often professional handlers augment their income by taking in boarding dogs. They must be able to purchase food and supplies in large quantities and estimate their needs from week to week, season to season.

Professional handlers are successful because they win. They must also be good at client relations. Handlers and their clients often establish long-term associations, but these need to be nurtured, just as any business must cater to its customers.

Handling is as much a people profession as it is a dog profession. Anyone contemplating this as a career needs to keep that facet of the business in mind.

KENNEL MANAGER

There are careers closely related to handling which do not actually involve going into the show ring. One of these is the job of kennel manager.

Most professional handlers who maintain a kennel, either solely for their show clients or for a combination of show and pet boarding, require a full-time, often live-in, kennel manager. This person is responsible for the day-to-day management of the dogs. The manager may be the only employee of the handler or he or she may be the supervisor of several full- or part-time people who do the actual work of scrubbing, bathing, feeding and all the other things which make a good kennel function well.

There are kennel manager positions for many other types of establishments, too. Many kennels only deal with pet boarding and some of these are very large, housing as many as two hundred dogs in a busy holiday season. There are commercial breeding kennels, also, which raise dogs for research. Although dog fanciers might not consider this ethically compatible with their interests, nonetheless these kennels and dogs need competent help, too.

From the early 1900s up to the end of World War II, many large private kennels were in existence. These kennels maintained as many as a hundred dogs which were bred and shown by kennel managers for their wealthy owners. Today there are very few private kennels of such magnitude, but there are some. These kennels housing one or two breeds usually employ a kennel manager who is capable of managing the kennel, whelping litters and caring for the young stock. They may also show the dogs, but often the top prospects are sent to professional handlers outside the kennel to be campaigned.

GROOMER

The grooming business can be lucrative for anyone interested pursuing a career in dogs. A professional groomer is in demand in the more populated urban or suburban areas. Grooming shops do well in shopping malls or in locations convenient to people's travels. There is also a growing demand for mobile groomers, who will go to a client's home and bathe, trim and groom dogs on the premises. There are vehicles professionally equipped to serve this business. Some professional groomers establish relationships with kennels that board pets so that every pet leaves the kennel clean and groomed. Many veterinarians employ groomers part-time. A regular grooming shop would do well near either of these establishments, also.

There are schools which teach grooming techniques, almost exclusively for pet grooming. The experience of working with many different breeds is invaluable, however. It is beneficial to know how to groom both pet and show dogs and the different methods employed for each.

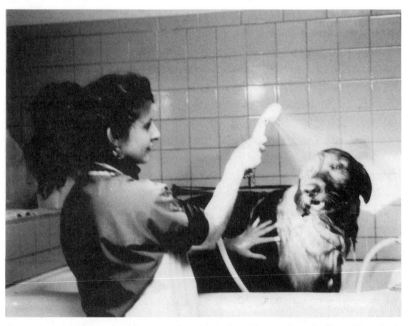

A groomer must know how to recognize signs of problems when dealing with a dog's skin and coat. Individual breed knowledge is also very helpful in making a dog look its best.

VETERINARY TECHNICIAN

Veterinary technicians are the most valuable asset a veterinarian has in practice. The vet tech is trained through two years of school to do almost everything that a veterinarian can do except surgery, diagnosis of illness and prescription of medication. Veterinary technicians assist in the operating room, can give vaccinations, care for the animals in the hospital, work in the pharmacy and deal generally with the animals and their owners. It is a growing field and one that so far has been underutilized by the veterinary profession.

There are several colleges throughout the United States which offer degrees for veterinary technicians. The American Veterinary Medical Association (see ''Useful Addresses'' in the appendix) can supply a list of accredited schools in the United States and Canada.

OFFICE MANAGER

A related position to the technician is that of office manager in a veterinary practice. Increasingly, veterinary practices are com-

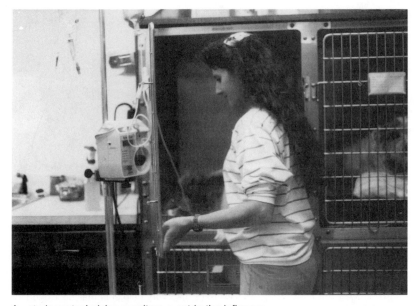

A veterinary technician monitors a cat in the infirmary.

145

Phone and computer skills are necessary for receptionist/office managers.

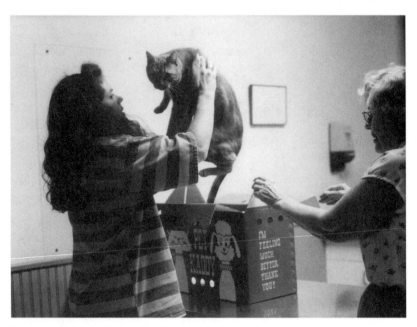

Sometimes they have to help with the patients and owners too.

prised of several veterinarians, often specialists in various fields. The office manager for a busy practice has the job of scheduling, purchasing, overseeing the help, taking care of all matters relating to payroll, accounting and billing. This position does not require veterinary training, but a knowledge of the profession, a love of animals and an ability to handle clients is necessary for success in this type of job.

VETERINARIAN

Veterinarians are the dog owners' as well as the dogs' best friend. They are the health care providers for pets, the advisers to breeders and owners and at the forefront of scientific health advances for animals. They also protect the public from food-transmitted diseases. Veterinarians work in research laboratories, in the military, on ranches and farms and in zoos. They work in underdeveloped countries helping to raise the standards of domestic animal health. They are found in jungles and on the plains of Africa

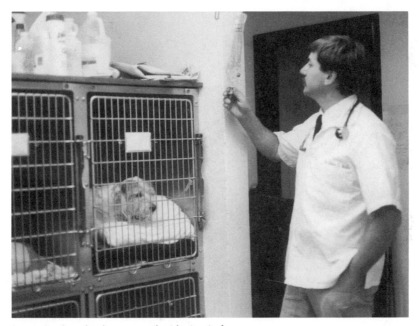

A veterinarian checks on a patient just out of surgery.

working with endangered species of animals and birds. They are increasingly found under the seas working with fish and marine mammals.

There are large-animal and small-animal veterinarians in private practice. There are veterinarians who specialize in birds or exotics. In other words, veterinary medicine is a field with many different avenues and opportunities for careers.

In order to be a veterinarian one must complete four years of college and four years of veterinary school. Then, if one wishes to specialize further, post-graduate education is necessary. Becoming a veterinarian is expensive and one must plan on many years of

In a busy office, the veterinarian and the receptionist have their own jobs to do, but they depend on each other.

loans, grants, part-time work and debt repayment before one will see real profit from this profession. Those who enter the field of veterinary medicine, however, do so because of their love of animals. It is among the most rewarding of the animal-related professions, and it requires the most dedication to get there.

Most veterinarians in the United States enter private practice following graduation, although there are many opportunities in public service, research and related fields. Some areas are overcrowded, others are in great need of veterinary service for both large and small animals.

Veterinary schools, for the most part, have more applicants (by about three to one) than they have room for. Women outnumber men in most of the twenty-seven veterinary schools in the United States. Undergraduates should have a good grounding in the physical sciences, biology, zoology and physics, before applying to veterinary school. They must have above-average grades to be accepted in most of them. Many veterinary schools are regional, in that they are committed to accept students first from their own or surrounding states. This limits the number of openings available for out-of-state students. Work experience in a veterinary clinic is often helpful when applying. Such experience usually involves cleaning cages, bathing animals and doing other chores in the hospital during vacations and at other times when possible.

The American Veterinary Medical Association can provide a list of all the veterinary schools in the United States and Canada. Anyone who is interested in this field as a career should contact the schools early in their undergraduate years so that they will be able to take the required courses before applying to veterinary school.

TRAINER

Dog trainers and animal behaviorists are two related and growing fields. The dog-owning public is becoming more aware of the need for good companions and well-behaved pets. Many people, however, have no idea how to achieve these goals. In order to keep dogs in apartments, condos or suburban houses they have come to realize that their dogs have to be good neighbors and so they are turning to professional trainers to help them. This is a field in which

Dog trainers hold classes and seminars for dogs of all breeds and their owners.

anyone can hang out a sign and call himself or herself a trainer or an animal behaviorist. There are many schools for dog training, but none to train the trainers. There are many behaviorists, all with differing personal theories on why animals behave in certain ways, but there is no standard for performance. Unfortunately, therefore, many people who call themselves animal behaviorists lack sufficient background in animals, behavior or both.

Animal behaviorists, in particular, form and reform their own ideas based on personal experience. There are a few veterinary schools which have behaviorists on their staffs who teach the theories of why dogs and cats act the way they do in various situations.

A career in dog training or behavior counseling requires very personal experience in working with dogs in these areas. Obedience classes, training sessions and seminars are all necessary preparation. To be a true animal behaviorist involves a veterinary degree and further study in animal psychology in order to really become an expert. In addition, courses in human psychology would be needed because many of the problems seen in dogs and cats are directly related to their interactions with people.

MILITARY SERVICE

Working with animals as part of the military establishment offers benefits and training which are hard to duplicate anywhere. Military life is not for everyone, but for those who are willing to combine service in the armed forces with training and experience as a veterinary technician, it is an inviting option.

The United States Army Veterinary Service is composed of four basic divisions. Veterinary Corps officers are graduate doctors of veterinary medicine. Animal care specialists can work in any aspect of animal care in the Department of Defense. The veterinary services technician is a warrant officer who specializes in food hygiene, safety and quality assurance programs maintained by the army. Finally, the veterinary food inspection specialist is responsible for ensuring that supplies for the troops are wholesome and up to standards.

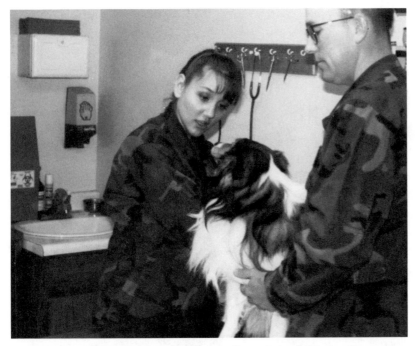

A veterinarian and a technician examine a family pet belonging to a military officer. Clinics are established at many military bases where military families live.
(Photo by William Wade, LVT, LATg, SFC, U.S. Army)

To become a veterinary technician in the armed forces one first goes through basic training. Those accepted for specialized veterinary training go on to the Animal Care Specialist School in Washington, D.C. This is a nine-week intensive course, after which inductees are assigned to a specialty. Soldiers who serve for two years and are promoted in rank may be selected to attend the Advanced Animal Care Specialist course which prepares students for advanced technical skills as trainers and teachers.

Members of the veterinary corps may be assigned to work in treatment facilities at installations worldwide. All veterinary services are administered by the Department of Defense, which staffs army, air force, navy, marine or Coast Guard bases. These installations are comparable to small animal clinics in private practice.

Depending on the location, the range of duties for military veterinary technicians varies from working with pets to exotic species. Some technicians are trained to work with laboratory animals, from rodents to primates. The army maintains one of the most

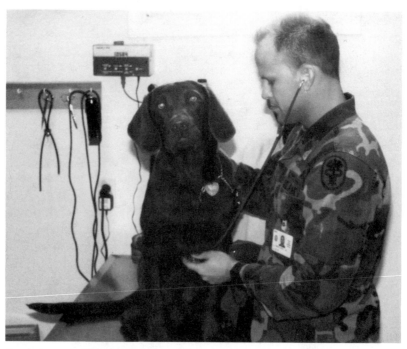

A veterinary specialist examines a military dog in a routine check up.
(Photo by William Wade, LVT, LATg, SFC, U.S. Army)

152

advanced biomedical research facilities in the world, and those selected for this duty can gain excellent experience working with
animals.

Military technicians have been sent to assist in rescuing animals
caught in hurricanes and floods, as well as being responsible for
dogs on active duty around the world. It is one of the interesting
professions which can combine a career with love of animals for
those willing and able to take advantage of the opportunities afforded
by the armed forces.

Participation in Junior Showmanship can open up avenues of
endeavor which are varied and challenging. The lessons learned by
young people both in and out of the show ring can be applied in any
number of ways to the choice of a career involving animals.

Former Junior handler and retired professional handler, George Alston, lectures and demonstrates for aspiring handlers and owner/exhibitors at clinics throughout the United States.

13

Giving Something Back

THROUGH THE YEARS in which young people have participated in Junior Showmanship, they have benefited from the counsel of friends and family. They have made lasting friendships through friendly competition and shared interests. They have learned the values of sportsmanship, responsibility and patience, and the physical coordination which makes a good performer.

Once they are out of Juniors they have an opportunity to give something back to the sport which has engaged them during the years they have been growing up. They can do this by sharing their knowledge and experience with youngsters starting out.

Juniors can take a newcomer under their wing, so to speak, and act as a mentor or teacher to the young hopefuls starting out. This can be done individually on a one-to-one basis, or it can be done by organizing small classes in your community for young people interested in dogs. Possibly a local kennel club would welcome an offer to teach Juniors by one who has had the personal experience in competition.

Juniors can offer their experiences to local schools to help educate children on the care and responsibilities of owning and enjoying a pet. The American Kennel Club has an extensive program geared especially to elementary school children. This would be an ideal opportunity for young people to talk to those just beginning.

There is another important way to give something back to the sport. That is by becoming a Junior Showmanship judge. Once Juniors are out of competition at the age of eighteen, they become eligible to be granted Junior Showmanship judging approval. They will have to go through the approval process, which involves applying to AKC to judge Juniors, filling out the application and being interviewed by a staff member at AKC. Once they are approved they may be asked to judge all Junior Showmanship classes at all-breed and Specialty shows.

Junior Showmanship judges are treated the same as any other judge. They may be paid a fee or reimbursed for expenses. Their contractual agreements with the show-giving club are the same as conformation or Obedience judges. They are listed in the premium lists and catalogs and they are expected to abide by the same rules of conduct and etiquette as any other judge.

The intimate knowledge that former Juniors bring to judging, however, makes them uniquely equipped to undertake this important task. It is the best tribute they can pay to the sport which has sustained them throughout their formative years.

Glossary

All-breed club. A group of fanciers representing different breeds that have organized into a club to protect and promote the interests of pure-bred dogs. These clubs put on shows and conduct educational programs for the general public as well as exhibitors and breeders. They often hold classes for show or Obedience training.

American Kennel Club. The largest registry body for pure-bred dogs in the world. In addition to registering dogs, keeping the Stud Books and breeding records of *every* registered dog, AKC is the governing body for *all* AKC events. These include dog shows, Field Trials, Obedience Trials, Lure Coursing, Herding and Tracking Trials. AKC keeps records on every dog which has been awarded points at licensed AKC shows and issues champion certificates for those dogs who have completed the championship requirements in conformation, Obedience or Field.

AKC approves judges for all breeds, Obedience Trials and Junior Showmanship. AKC publishes a monthly magazine, *Pure-Bred Dogs, AKC Gazette*, which contains articles of interest to the dog Fancy. A companion magazine lists all approved shows and events several months in advance. A separate publication records all points awarded to dogs in every breed in competition.

AKC also maintains a large library of books and videos. Videos are available for purchase. The library is a resource center for every facet of dogs and dog care. AKC maintains a field staff which attends almost every show, Obedience and Field Trial throughout the United States. It also maintains an investigations staff whose responsibility is to assure that breeders keep accurate records and to work with local enforcement officials should they find evidence of inhumane treatment of animals.

AKC is composed of member clubs. There are no individual members of AKC. Member clubs appoint or elect Delegates to represent them to the AKC at quarterly meetings. Delegates are charged with the responsibility of electing the AKC Board of Directors, which, in turn, hires a President to act as chief of staff. The Board of Directors is responsible for setting policy for the kennel club. The staff is responsible for carrying out those policies.

Back. In anatomical terms, the back of the dog is that portion of the topline starting just behind the withers and ending at the beginning of the loin.

Bait. Bait is considered to be anything which is used by handlers in the show ring to animate dogs so they look alert and interested. Many handlers use small pieces of dried liver which dogs like and which are easy to carry in a "bait pocket." Balls, squeaky toys, other types of favorite foods can also be used. Some breeds are customarily shown "free-baited." This means that the dog is trained to stand perfectly without the handler physically placing the feet, head or tail in position. The handler then uses bait to keep attention focused so that the dog maintains the correct stance before and after the judge performs the examination.

Barrel-chested. A configuration in many breeds having a chest in which the ribs are rounded. Sometimes this pushes the elbows out from the sides of the body, and in Bulldogs this conformation is acceptable. In many other breeds it is considered a fault.

Benched show. There are two types of shows: benched and unbenched. A benched show is one at which dogs are required to be present during specified hours and remain at designated stalls at all times unless it is actually in the ring, being prepared to be shown or being exercised. Stalls are compartments raised off the ground and separated by sections. Dogs are benched together according to breed and group in most instances. In the early days of dog shows all shows were benched, but now fewer than a half dozen are. This is because of the additional space needed and the added expense to the clubs of erecting benches. It is also because most exhibitors prefer the convenience of showing their dogs and leaving.

Unbenched shows are those at which exhibitors may arrive at any time before their breeds are being judged and may leave directly after judging. Although this is convenient for the exhibitor, it does not afford spectators the opportunity of seeing all the breeds that may be present at some time during the day. It also does not afford the educational opportunities that occur when exhibitors exchange information "on the bench."

Best of Breed. The dog or bitch selected by the judge to be the overall winner among all the dogs within one breed at a given show.

Best in Show. The dog or bitch selected to be the overall winner among all the dogs in competition at a show. This term should be reserved for dogs that win at all-breed shows. The dog that wins Best at a Specialty show is properly called Best of Breed or a Specialty Best of Breed winner, as Specialties are one-breed shows.

Best of Winners. The award given to either Winners Dog or Winners Bitch in each breed at a show.

Bitch. The female of the species. In dog show terminology, all females are bitches and all males are referred to as dogs.

Bite. The term given to the position of the upper and lower teeth in relation to each other. The judge will ask an exhibitor to "show the bite." This means the exhibitor holds the mouth slightly open so that the judge can see if the bite is correct. Some breeds require that the judge examine the whole mouth to see if there are missing teeth. There are three main types of bites: *scissors bite*, in which the upper teeth fit closely over the lower; *level bite*, in which the front teeth meet together evenly; *undershot bite*, in which the lower teeth protrude beyond but may not meet the upper. Most breed Standards specify which types of bite are acceptable or preferred. Another type of bite is the *overshot bite*, in which the upper teeth protrude far beyond the lower. This is a fault in every breed.

Bloat. This is a disease of the stomach in which the stomach fills with gas and sometimes twists in the abdominal cavity. The medical term is gastric dilatation volvulus (GDV) and is always an emergency. Large, deep-chested dogs are at greatest risk.

Carpus. This is usually called the wrist and is the joint between the forearm and the pastern on the front leg.

Catalog. A publication required of a club at every show which lists every dog entered by breed and class. Catalog listings include the dog's AKC registry number, names of sire and dam, date of birth, sex, breeder, owner and handler. Catalogs are customarily sold on the show grounds.

Champion. The title conferred upon a dog who completes the AKC requirements of earning fifteen points, including two shows at which three points or more are awarded under different judges.

Conformation. The conformation of a dog is the way it looks, its appearance and movement. Dog shows are an evaluation of a dog's conformation, as distinct from Obedience Trials or Junior Showmanship in which conformation is not judged.

Courtesy turn. The position into which a Junior Handler moves before setting out on an individual gaiting pattern. The courtesy turn takes the exhibitor in front of the judge and turns the dog toward the judge before moving down the ring.

Cowhocks. Hocks which turn inward from the perpendicular, indicating a weakness in the joints.

Croup. The area just in front of the set-on of the tail from the hip joint to the buttocks.

Dam. The mother of a litter of puppies.

Dog. In dog show terminology a dog is the male of the species, as distinct from a bitch, which is the female.

External parasites. Pests which infest the coat and skin. The most common of these are fleas and ticks. There are, however, other parasites, such as mange mites, lice, scabies and chiggers, which are sometimes seen, depending upon the region of the country in which you live.

Flank. The area of the body between the end of the abdomen behind the rib cage and the hindquarters.

Gait/gaiting. Gait is the way a dog moves. To gait in the show ring is to move the dog at a steady pace, usually a trot, away from and back to the judge so the judge can see the dog going away, sideways and coming to the front. A gaiting pattern is the direction which the judge requests a handler to move in order that the gait be properly displayed. In Junior Showmanship learning to gait the dog so that it looks its best while moving is one of the most important elements of exhibiting the dog.

Groups. The seven categories of dogs recognized by AKC which are eligible to compete in AKC shows. They are: Sporting, Hound, Terrier, Working, Toy, Non-Sporting and Herding. There are 136 breeds divided into these seven groups.

Hip dysplasia. A hereditary condition in which the head of the femur (the hip bone) does not fit securely into the acetabulum (the hip socket). This may cause pain, lameness and eventually arthritis.

Hock/hock joint. The hock is technically a joint which connects the lower thigh and the rear pastern. It is correctly called a hock joint, although the term "hock" is used to describe the rear pastern.

Infertility. The inability of a dog to produce viable sperm or a bitch to conceive puppies.

Internal parasites. Worms or bacteria which are found inside the animal. The most common are intestinal worms, such as hook, whip, tape and round. Heartworm is another internal parasite which affects the heart and lungs. The spirochete which causes Lyme disease is an internal bacterium which can affect any part of the body.

Judging schedule. The listing at every show of all judges, the breeds they are scheduled to judge, the number of dogs of each breed entered, the ring numbers and the estimated times each breed is to be judged. The judging schedule also lists the number of entrants in each Junior Showmanship class, the judge or judges for those classes, the ring number and the estimated time for judging to begin.

Lead. A lead is any type of leash or leash and collar combination which is used to control a dog in the show ring. There are many types of leads and most exhibitors experiment with several before finding the one best suited to the dog.

Mandible. The lower jaw or underjaw in anatomical terms.

Match show. A show at which no championship points are awarded. Match shows are generally practice shows for young and inexperienced dogs. It is a training opportunity for inexperienced handlers as well. Entry fees are lower than at point shows and entries usually smaller. Many Match shows do not require preentry, although there are some which must be preentered. Match shows are like scrimmages, they simulate the real thing but do not count for points toward any title.

Muzzle. The portion of the head which is in front of the skull including the upper and lower jaws.

Neck. The section of the body between the head and shoulders. The neck is part of the topline of the dog.

Parent Club. The national organization representing fanciers of any particular breed. Most Parent Clubs are members of the American Kennel Club and are represented by a Delegate. These clubs put on National Specialties or other events, depending upon the breeds. They disseminate information about their breeds and their charters usually state that their purpose is to protect and promote their breeds.

162

Parvovirus. A highly contagious intestinal disease which causes acute diarrhea, vomiting, fever, weakness and sometimes death, especially in young puppies. It is effectively controlled by vaccination.

Pastern. The region between the wrist and the foot on both front and rear legs. Rear leg pasterns are sometimes called the hocks, although this is incorrect.

Pedigree. The pedigree of a dog is the written ancestry of that dog for at least three generations. The pedigree lists the parents, grandparents and great-grandparents. This is a three-generation pedigree. Often pedigrees include a fourth, fifth or sixth generation.

Pelvis/pelvic joint. The pelvis is composed of three bones and is the main part of the hindquarters. These are joined to each other and to the hip socket.

Point show. A point show is one at which championship points are awarded in every breed. The number of points in each breed is determined by the number of dogs in actual competition in that breed. The number of points ranges from one to five and varies according to the region of the country in which the shows are held. AKC annually fixes the point schedule according to seven regions within the United States, plus Hawaii and Puerto Rico. Winners Dog and Winners Bitch in each breed are awarded the points at conformation shows. (See ''How a Show Is Organized'' in the appendix.)

Premium list. This is the entry information and form which is sent out by the club Secretary or Superintendent for a show. The premium list gives the name of the show, date, classes offered, prizes to be awarded, directions to the show's site, entry fees and the closing date (the last date on which entries can be accepted for that show).

Professional Handlers Association (PHA). The main professional organization which represents people whose exclusive income is derived from handling dogs. This organization has strict requirements for membership and is national in scope.

Purebred. A pure-bred dog is one which is traceable through its pedigree for at least three generations in which all the antecedents are verifiably of the same breed. AKC will only recognize as purebred those dogs which meet this requirement. There are breeds which are purebred, however, but not recognized by AKC. Worldwide there are approximately four hundred breeds recognized in various countries throughout the world. AKC recognizes 136.

Registration. A dog's registration is certification by AKC that it is a pure-bred dog. *AKC registration does not indicate quality.*

Scapula. The anatomical term for shoulder blade, which is the wide, flat bone which at the top forms the withers and is attached by muscles and ligaments to the first ribs and at the base to the front leg bone. This is called the point of the shoulder or prosternum.

Sire. The father of the litter.

Skull. The portion of the head in back of the muzzle which contains the brain.

Slab-sided. Ribs which are flat, so that the dog when seen from above shows no roundness to the sides. In some breeds, such as the Borzoi, this is correct when corresponding to a very deep chest. In other breeds it is considered a fault.

Snipey. Elongation and narrowness in the muzzle of a breed which is not supposed to have that characteristic.

Stack/stacking. In the show ring when a dog is standing properly according to the fashion of the breed it is considered to be in a stack, or has been stacked by the handler. Many breeds are stacked by the exhibitor who positions the head, feet, body and tail and who either stands or kneels next to the dog on the ground or positions the dog on an examining table. A dog which is free-stacked positions itself and is expected to hold that position. These breeds are free-baited to achieve that position. (See **Bait**.)

Specialty club. A club of fanciers of one breed only. This can be a Parent Club, which is national in scope, or a local or regional club. The events and purposes are the same.

Specialty show. A Specialty is a show held for one breed only. It can be run by a local breed club of a national Parent Club for the breed. All classes held at all-breed shows are customarily offered at Specialties. There may be other classes for Juniors, for Veterans or special features, depending upon the breeds.

Standard. Every recognized AKC breed must have a written Standard of perfection for that breed. These are the descriptions of the breeds by which dogs are judged. Standards are developed by the Parent Clubs for each breed and are considered to be the definitive words describing those breeds. Judges are expected to award ribbons to those dogs which most closely fit the Standard for the breed they represent.

Steward. Every ring at a dog show is expected to have at least one, and preferably two, stewards. The duties of the steward are to assist the judge in all respects except for judging and marking the judges' books. Stewards dispense armbands at ringside, which are the only identification an exhibitor wears. They call the classes to the ring according to the judges' instructions. They keep track of exhibitors, present and absent. They organize the ribbons and prizes according to classes and lay them out to help the judges dispense them at the conclusion of each class. Stewards have been known to come to the rescue of exhibitors whose buttons have popped, hems have dropped or leads have snapped. Sometimes they save a judge embarrassment by pointing out missed exhibitors or mismarked books. Good stewards are invaluable to the smooth running of a show.

Stifle joint. The joint which connects the upper and lower thighs of the hind leg. Hindquarter angulation is determined by the angle formed at this joint. A somewhat common orthopedic problem, slipping stifles, also involves this joint.

Stop. The bony rise between the muzzle and the skull. The appearance of the head is greatly influenced by the stop. Some are very definite, such as a Setter, and others are almost nonexistent, such as the Collie.

Superintendent. There are several business organizations whose function is to handle all the details of running a show. They send out premium lists, publish the catalog, organize the judges' schedules and provide the rings to be set up, tenting to be secured for outdoor shows and ribbons and judges' books for every class. They also record every win and send the results to AKC.

Superintendents do not choose the judges, provide trophies, clean up or any of the millions of other details which go into making a successful show. They are, however, the providers of the nuts and bolts. They perform these services for a fee. Some clubs superintend their own shows and use a show Secretary to take care of all the paperwork. This is usually the case for Specialty shows. All-breed shows most often use Superintendents.

Sweepstakes. Classes which are held for puppies and young dogs at Specialty shows, usually between the ages of six and eighteen months. Cash prizes are awarded at Sweepstakes depending upon the number of entries in each class.

Topline. The topline is the dog's outline from the head to the tail when you look at the dog from the side.

Type. Characteristics of anatomy and expression which distinguish one breed from another.

Vaccinations. Inoculations given to dogs to prevent them from contracting some of the more serious illnesses. Puppies are customarily vaccinated three or four times for distemper, hepatitis, parainfluenza and parvovirus and twice for leptospirosis. These are often all given in a single combination vaccine starting when the puppies are six or seven weeks old. When they are a year old they should have annual booster vaccinations. All dogs should be vaccinated against rabies when they are puppies and again every two years. In most states rabies vaccinations are the law.

Vertebrae. A line of bones, sometimes called the spinal column, which runs from the head down to the end of the tail. The spinal column contains the central nervous system.

Winners Bitch. The bitch selected as the best non-champion female in regular class competition at a given show. She is the only female winner of points in her breed that day.

Winners Dog. The dog selected as the best non-champion male in regular class competition at a given show. He is the only male winner of points in his breed that day.

Withers. The point at which the shoulder blades come close together at their tips on either side of the spinal column. The point at which a measuring device may be placed to determine a dog's height.

Appendices

How a Show Is Organized

Taken from *Regulations Judging Guidelines and Guidelines for Juniors:*

BEST IN SHOW

GROUP COMPETITION

(Sporting, Hound, Working, Terrier, Toy, Non-Sporting, Herding)

BREED COMPETITION

Best of Breed

Best of Opposite Sex

Best of Winners

Winners Dog (receives points)	Winners Bitch (receives points)
Reserve Winners Dog	Reserve Winners Bitch
Open Dog	Open Bitch
American Bred Dog	American Bred Bitch
Bred-by-Exhibitor Dog	Bred-by-Exhibitor Bitch
Novice Dog	Novice Bitch
Puppy Dog	Puppy Bitch

(Sometimes Puppy classes are divided by age into 6–9 months and 9–12 months.)

Clubs may offer other classes, such as Veteran Dog and

169

Veteran Bitch, which may be divided by age. Customarily, nonregular classes such as these are offered at Specialty shows.

Useful Addresses

American Kennel Club
51 Madison Avenue
New York, NY 10010

American Veterinary Medical Association
1931 North Meacham Road
Suite 100
Schaumburg, IL 60173

North American Veterinary Technicians Association (NAVTA)
1904 West 107th Street
First Floor
Chicago, IL 60643

Westminster Kennel Club
230 Park Avenue
Room 644
New York, NY 10169

Dog Show Superintendents

William Antypas
P.O. Box 7131
Pasadena, CA 91109

Jack Bradshaw
P.O. Box 7303
Los Angeles, CA 90022

Norman Brown
P.O. Box 2566
Spokane, WA 99220

Thomas Crowe
P.O. Box 22107
Greensboro, NC 27420

Helen Houser
P.O. Box 420
Quakertown, PA 18951

Ace Mathews
P.O. Box 86130
Portland, OR 97286

Moss-Bow
P.O. Box 22107
Greensboro, NC 27420

Newport Dog Shows
P.O. Box 7131
Pasadena, CA 91109

Jack Onofrio
P.O. Box 25764
Oklahoma City, OK 73125

Bob Peters
P.O. Box 579
Wake Forest, NC 27588

James Rau, Jr.
P.O. Box 6898
Reading, PA 19610

Kenneth Sleeper
P.O. Box 828
Auburn, IN 46706

Classes Offered for Juniors at Conformation Shows

Novice Junior For boys and girls who are at least ten but under fourteen years of age on the day of the show who, at the time entries close, have not won three First Place awards, with competition present, in a Novice class at a licensed or member show.

Novice Senior For boys and girls who are at least fourteen but under eighteen years of age on the day of the show who, at the time entries close, have not won three First Place awards, with competition present, in a Novice class at a licensed or member show.

Open Junior For boys and girls who are at least ten but under fourteen years of age on the day of the show who have won three First Place awards in a Novice class in a licensed or member show, with competition present. The winner of a Novice class shall automatically become eligible, upon notice to the Open class ring steward, to enter and compete in the Open class at the same show, provided the win is the third First Place award with competition and further providing there are one or more Junior Handlers competing in the Open class.

Open Senior For boys and girls who are at least fourteen but under eighteen years of age on the day of the show who have won three First Place awards in a Novice class in a licensed or member show, with competition present. The winner of the Novice class shall automatically become eligible, upon notice to the Open class ring steward, to enter and compete in the Open class at the same show provided the win is the third First Place award with competition and further providing there are one or more Junior Handlers competing in the Open class.

Best Junior Handler A club offering Junior Showmanship may offer a prize for Best Junior Handler. The Junior Handler placed first in each of the regular Junior Showmanship classes, if undefeated in any other Junior Showmanship class at that show, shall automatically be eligible to compete for this prize.

172

Bibliography

Books

Alston, G. G., and C. Vanacore. *The Winning Edge, Show Ring Secrets*. New York: Howell Book House, 1992.

American Kennel Club. *The Complete Dog Book*. New York: Howell Book House, 1992. A comprehensive, illustrated look at every registerable breed in the AKC Stud Book. Includes a chapter on health care and puppy training.

Benjamin, Carol Lea. *Mother Knows Best: The Natural Way to Train Your Dog*. New York: Howell Book House, 1985. A readable, commonsense approach to teaching basic manners and solving problems. Written with humor in simple language.

Carlson, D. G., DVM, and J. Giffin, MD. *Dog Owner's Home Veterinary Handbook*. New York: Howell Book House, 1992.

Kay, William J., DVM. *The Complete Book of Dog Health*. New York: Howell Book House, Macmillan, 1985. Chief of staff at the Animal Medical Center, New York, gives detailed descriptions of the major internal systems of the dog and describes common ailments which owners can identify.

McGinnis, Terri, DVM. *The Well Dog Book*. New York: Random House, 1991. A basic veterinary manual for dog owners; describes what is normal and what is abnormal. For example, what is the normal temperature for a dog and when to worry.

Spira, Harry, DVM. *Canine Terminology*. New York: Howell Book House, 1982. The definitive description of canine anatomy from A to Z, from nose to tail, arranged with illustrations in alphabetical order.

Taylor, David, DVM, and Connie Vanacore. *The Ultimate Dog Book*. New York: Simon & Schuster, 1990. A lavishly illustrated description of most of the breeds registered in the United States and Great Britain.

Vanacore, Connie. *Dog Showing: An Owner's Guide*. New York: Howell Book House, 1991. A step-by-step tour through the conformation ring written for the novice exhibitor.

Volhard, Jack, and Melissa Bartlett. *What All Good Dogs Should Know*. New York: Howell Book House, 1991. A basic primer for Obedience training, giving simple reasons for why some techniques work better than others.

Periodicals

Pure-Bred Dogs, American Kennel Gazette. The official publication of the American Kennel Club. Published monthly. Contains articles of interest to the Fancy. A separate magazine is included listing all events for the following several months. Another monthly publication, *The Awards Section*, may be purchased as part of a subscription listing awards given at dog shows, Obedience Trials, Field Trials, Hunting Trials, Herding and Lure Coursing events.

Note: Many books have been published on individual breeds. Your local library or bookstore can tell you whether there is a book available on your chosen breed.

Parent Clubs often publish monthly, bi-monthly or quarterly magazines or newsletters giving interesting information about the breeds, upcoming events, seminars and Specialty shows. You can learn a great deal by reading the club's publications before and after you purchase a puppy.

Index